The Theatrical Image

JAMES H. CLAY

Brandeis University

DANIEL KREMPEL

Syracuse University

MCGRAW-HILL BOOK COMPANY

New York, St. Louis, San Francisco,

Toronto, London, Sydney

The Theatrical Image

Library of Congress Catalog Card Number 67-12619

11286

1234567890 HD 7432106987

For Joyce and Delight

Preface

What I cannot defend, unless you are willing to grant it, is the value of form as the kind of experience that goes most deeply into whatever a man is. Dance, ritual, religious ceremony, public ceremony or poetic encounter—if the form is sound, it is of what is deepest in man. Nothing is more powerfully of man than the fact that he naturally gives off forms and is naturally enclosed by them. To acquire knowledge of aesthetic form is to acquire knowledge of man.

John Ciardi[1]

The theory of theatrical form upon which this book is based implies more clearly than anything else the primacy of intuitive genius in the creation of art. But genius is neither a profession nor a craft, and even the great mind must find specific ways of working, principles and procedures which make its creativity effective. On the surface, such procedures are merely skills and craftsmanship, but at heart, the working habits of the artist are inevitably bound up in concepts. By hard-won experience, the actor, the playwright, the director, or the designer can tell when a certain effect is "right" or "wrong"—and so, though he may not realize it, his craftsmanship depends on an *idea* of what theatrical art is and how it works.

This is not a book about how to direct a play, how to act it, or how to design it. It will not tell you how many rehearsals to hold or how to make working drawings or scenery. It does come to grips with the truly practical problems that are prior to and deeper than such procedures as casting, scheduling, and designing. The first questions put are the ultimately practical ones: not "What does the play mean?" but "What kind of meaning does a play *create?*" and "*How* does it have meaning?" Having answered that, this book moves from a definition of how theatre creates its effects to the working methods that the definition implies.

Do the techniques in common use by theatre artists seem to be related in any way to the kind of meaning which is termed "dramatic"? If so, are there other, related, techniques which might be profitably employed? What are the dangers of such theory-based approaches? In considering these and similar questions, this book offers an organized statement of the working methods inherent in the very nature of theatrical art—ways of working which, since they grow out of the dynamics of the medium, are potentially the most creative approaches to interpreting plays for performance.

Craftsmanship depends on an idea of what theatrical art is and how it works. This is a book about such ideas.

James H. Clay
Daniel Krempel

Acknowledgments

For valuable criticism of various drafts of the manuscript, we are indebted to Professor Barnard Hewitt of the University of Illinois, Professor and Mrs. Ray Ginger of the Brandeis University History Department, and Professor John Matthews of the Brandeis Theatre Arts Department.

In other categories of assistance, Professor Karl Wallace of the University of Illinois contributed to the initiation of the work; the administration of Brandeis University gave generous help with problems of researching photographs and preparing the manuscript; also helpful were Professor Louis Kronenberger of Brandeis, Helen Willard of the Harvard Theatre Collection, directors William Ball and Tyrone Guthrie, and designers Frederick Crooke and Lester Polakov.

Since our debt to Mordecai Gorelik is a special one, it is described in the essay on sources, which appears at the back of the book.

Contents

List of Photographs

The Theatrical Image

If you are afraid of the seriousness of a play you "stylise" it.

MICHEL SAINT-DENIS[2]

INTRODUCTION: **The Problem**

From the beginning until the latter half of the nineteenth century every major period of theatre art had what we now call a style. Most theatre workers in any one of these periods produced plays according to a traditional pattern, which was the only conceivable one for the time.

However, like all the arts today, our theatre is totally unlike those of the past in the degree of its self-consciousness, its awareness, and its concern with matters of "style." After 1880, the theatre presents an almost bewildering array of movements, modes, countermovements, and manners.

For example, during the last half century Shakespeare's *Macbeth* has been seen in these forms:

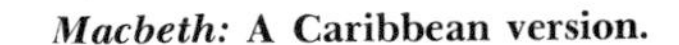

***Macbeth:* A Caribbean version.**

4

***Macbeth:* A theatre school production.**

5

Macbeth: Highly stylized costumes.

Macbeth: A New Stagecraft interpretation.

6

And here are four *Hamlets* of our era . . .

7

8

9

10

This century has seen *Hamlet* performed as:

A drawing-room drama, in modern evening dress, about a nervous young man

A drama of homosexual affection between Hamlet and Horatio

An Oedipus-complex psychodrama

An atom-age play of split personalities, with separate Hamlets, Gertrudes, and Claudii for each split of these characters

An economic-determinist tract about castle intrigue and power politics

A series of lovely poetic recitations with intermittent movement in moody sets, lights, costumes, and music

And as a Graustarkian melodrama in the costumes of *The Student Prince*

Such strange variation in the presentation of a single playscript is a phenomenon unique to the modern theatre. This exploding pattern has some wonderfully stimulating aspects, but it makes matters of artistic judgment peculiarly difficult in our time.

Historically, the manner of execution in art becomes a primary concern when the importance of content wanes. When the culture or person is afire with feelings or ideas, ways are found to execute those ideas; the manner of execution is less important than getting the thing said.

Indeed, the manner grows quite naturally out of the ideas. In time the enthusiasm wears off, however, and the person or culture settles comfortably into its newfound notions. These ideas are served up again and again until they become flat and tasteless, and thus we find a growing concern with the way the dish is prepared rather than with its basic ingredient. Artists labor at perfecting technique or exploring new modes of preparation and decoration of what were once vital messages to be delivered without affectation. We seem to be in such a period now.

The once vital idea of artistic freedom has been perverted to mean artistic license, and reasonable criticism has been labeled dangerous censorship hampering creativity. The result is an atmosphere of strained politeness in which one feels obliged to "appreciate" everything and embarrassed to criticize anything.

> **And now, at last, triumphant amid the debris of centuries of tradition, liberated from every convention, supported by a public that will tolerate anything provided it has not been done before, the artist finds himself in the happy position of being able to thumb his nose at the world. It is a gesture that is a little more difficult to perform on the stage than elsewhere, but it can be done—is done, in fact —every day with varying degrees of grace.**
>
> *Maurice Valency*[11]

One result in the theatre has been a chaos of stylizations too easily rationalized by the contention that a play means different things to different people and that arguments over correctness of interpretation are therefore pointless. In the frantic search for originality in theatrical production, the content of the production—the meaning of the play—is too often disregarded. The seductions of the bright idea, the clever twist, the "Nobody has ever tried . . . !" too often pervert the potentially healthy production into an artificially propelled freak. We have even reached the point of staging experimental productions just for the sake of being experimental.

***Troilus and Cressida:* Experimenting to find what?**

12

Why is it that no one seems to ask such questions? Perhaps because the struggle of nineteenth-century artists against the official aesthetics of the academies and traditionalist critics has succeeded all too well, with the result that hard-won freedom has now degenerated into art for the artist's sake.

Is there no right way to interpret a play? Through its

***King Lear:* To prove what?**

13

productions, the modern theatre seems to answer, "No." The present period tends to be one in which anything goes as long as it is "a good show."

Yet, though their work sometimes seems to belie their words, many important theatre artists would agree that the primary aim of a production should not be the self-expression of the performers, but a communication to the audience of the author's intent; thus:

Elia Kazan, at an ANTA assembly in which he denied rewriting *Cat on a Hot Tin Roof,* joined Albert Marre, Dore Schary, David Pressman, Alan Schneider, and Professor Willi Schmidt in stating:

The best director is the one who remains in the background and shuns both theatrical dogma and stylized direction. . . . Expressing the ruling sentiment of the discussion, Professor Schmidt of the Schiller and Schlosspark Theatres in Berlin said that the function of a director was to "bring life, with the help of his actors, to the lines written by the author."[14]

Max Reinhardt, referring to his Victorian, sugarplum-fairy film version of *A Midsummer Night's Dream,* said:

I have set the condition that this work should represent Shakespeare, and nothing but Shakespeare.[15]

Laurence Olivier, writing of his Freudian arrangement of *Hamlet,* stated:

My whole aim and purpose has been to make a film of* Hamlet *as Shakespeare himself, were he living now, might make it.[16]

Louis Jouvet made the most categorical affirmation of the principle, and apparently lived by it:

It is the author alone who is master in the theatre; he is the sole creator and his direction only is completely justified.[17]

All these statements imply that theatre art is a problem in communicating the author's intended meaning. But some artists object strongly, asserting that in many cases, especially in classic revivals, the author's intent is unknowable; still others react to "communication" with horrified objections to the notion that there are messages in art. Of course, to so strictly equate the word "communication" with the idea of a literal message in the propaganda sense is naïve. The message of a work of art *may* be a philosophical, political, or moral assertion; it may also be—and at the same time—simply a mood or a complex of feelings. All of these are messages to be communicated.

The chapter which follows approaches the all-important question, "What is the intended meaning?" by answering the more basic questions: "What is the nature of the message in a theatrical performance?" and "How does a play mean?"

Theory is born when practice becomes conscious,
for theory is nothing more than practice
carried on in the imagination.

GYORGY KEPES[1]

PART ONE: **How Does a Play Mean?**

The "meaning" contained in many a dramatic speech or chorus may be as direct as the "meaning" of a passage in Aristotle's *Ethics,* but that "meaning" which alone will explain the form of a play is something more akin to the "meaning" of a Rembrandt or of a Beethoven sonata.

***H. D. F. Kitto, Greek Tragedy*[2]**

You are dreaming.

A high barbed wire fence has been in your way, but you have succeeded in climbing through it. Now you must climb a jagged granite cliff. It is dark . . . treacherously so . . . yet you climb, carefully, slowly, tensely. You inch your way along, groping for the too slight handholds which you cannot see. The last few feet of cliff jut out into space above you like the edge of a giant table. Clutching, hanging, you strain higher and higher. At last you are able to stretch one arm up and over the top! Your hand claws at the loose dust on the flat top of the mountain . . . but there is nothing to hold on to—nothing to seize and so pull yourself over the edge to safety. You have maneuvered yourself into a position that you cannot cling to for more than a few seconds, yet the top is still inaccessible. Sweaty and gasping, you bolt into wakefulness—sit listening to the alarmed pounding of your heart. After a time, with the spell of the dream still upon you, sleep returns.

But the next morning the nightmare is still on your mind. You muse your way through it again, carefully, analytically. That barbed wire . . . you know that fence from somewhere. Of course! In every detail it was the one on the farm where you used to go hiking in your high school days. But the cliff? Where did it come from? It was granite. A very particular granite, greenish-gray . . . and old; in places rounded and scored by glacial ice, but near the summit, splintered and frost-rent, with wedges of it loose here and there so that a climber might fall if he were not terribly cautious. Suddenly you feel a surge of excitement—you know where *this* came from too. It was like the rock hills and mountains where you vacationed last summer. But the momentary pleasure of discovery fades. Odd, you think, that the dream's darkness was so deep that you could not see your hands clinging to the fissured rock, yet you remember the color and structure of the stone. Odder still, both the fence and the mountains were in reality the settings for very pleasant experiences, while in the dream they were terrifying.

Breakfast finds you still circling the dream, poking it here and there, but not finding its secret. The Freudians, you recall, would explain it as a series of symbols designed to mask socially inhibited desires. They would interpret the act of climbing as symbolic of the sex act—in this case an unsuccessful attempt at sexual conquest. You remember also the Freudian view that climbing up and down walls in a state of anxiety is supposed to represent that portion of one's infancy spent in climbing about on one's parents, smooth walls being Father and irregular walls being Mother. Intriguing. Very. But somehow not a sufficiently satisfying explanation. Only one thing seems certain—the nightmare followed a classical pattern of fear and frustration. Beyond that you cannot make it out, and so you try to put the whole business out of your mind.

But this single certainty—that the dream exhibits a common pattern of frustration and fear—is the one thing upon which almost all interpreters would agree. Perhaps such an observation should not be so quickly dismissed, merely because it is obvious. If one cannot pry open the mechanics of the dream to find out what particular desires and fears it represents, perhaps the broad principle of its function can nevertheless be discovered.

In attempting to riddle out his nightmare, the victim tried to relate the specific elements of his dream to real-life events. At first he supposed this dream was about particular happenings in his life, and the dream was therefore a literal recollection. Obviously, this was not a very fruitful supposition. The fence and the mountain were separated in his experience by 1,100 miles and eighteen years. Neither the granite nor the barbed wire was initially associated with struggle and foreboding, yet striving and doom made up the overpowering mood of the dream. Moreover, while the fence was a literal recollection, the dreamer had never climbed a cliff of any kind. Only the granite itself seemed purely from memory. Thus, the literal content of the dream offered no solution to its meaning.

Suppose now, that like the troubled author of the dream, we explore Freudian notions of its cause and meaning. If climbing the cliff is indeed a symbolic expression of the sex act and if such symbolism is necessary to conceal a socially inhibited activity, then we have found the answer. But if, as the dreamer preferred to think, this extremely common kind of dream does not necessarily refer to sex—what then? May not, with sufficient likelihood, dreams of climbing and falling refer to social and economic success, to the ego as well as the libido? Perhaps, but it is not necessary for our purposes to resolve this question.

The important thing is that whichever answer one chooses, he has operated with the same premise: *he has begun to think of the dream as a kind of metaphorical idea.* This is to say, the approximate message of the dream is construed as either "Mother is a cliff," or "My job is a cliff," or something of the sort. In both cases the meaning is metaphorical.

At this point one should be reminded that, at its best, metaphorical thinking creates new dimensions of feeling and understanding. It is a way of thinking which enables us to transfer appropriate and vivid emotional associations to a subject which we might not otherwise sense so keenly. A striking example is Macbeth's "My mind is full of scorpions." Instantly the nature of this vicious little animal, which hides in dark crevices, and all its hideous, loathsome, death-dealing characteristics are recalled; and when we associate this with the mind of Macbeth, his feelings are communicated to us with a visceral impact. But one should also recall that a metaphor which becomes a stock expression may in time lose its force altogether. Thus, "I'm swamped with work" carries no special vividness, and in an expression such as "the engine died" no emotional associations with actual death are even expected. Although a metaphor may fade in effect, essentially it is a device by which we obtain a deeper realization of some aspect of life.

Now, if one studies the nightmare example as metaphor—as emotional analogy—some of the puzzling matters are accounted for.[3] For one thing, the mingling of bits of reality and fiction can be understood since the exact sources for the parts of the metaphor are not important as long as they combine to produce the desired effect; therefore, the fact that the fence came from youthful memories of a definite place matters very little. What does matter in a metaphor expressing fear and frustration is that the feeling of danger and obstacles be created. Without question, the jagged cliff and the barbed wire create this feeling very well—well enough to awaken the dreamer in a frantic state. Apparently, fences and granite mountains were handily available to the sleeper's mind, and he made use of them in fabricating his dream. Depending on his background, he might have used barricades, ladders, roof tops, but in any case his aspirations and fears on that particular night would have found expression in such a pattern of dangerous obstacles. In sum, whether we accept or reject the Freudian view, we seem to be left with the idea that dreams are a kind of symbolism and that a metaphorical principle is involved.

According to such a view, the nightmare in question is not so much a matter of symbols in a series as it is one symbol in overall structure. That is, the total accumulation of events in the nightmare creates a feeling which parallels the complex of wishes and anxieties which besets the dreamer in real life. True, the fence and the cliff may be discussed profitably as separate symbols, but in final effect they are separate facets of the same device, in the same way that there is more than one scorpion, more than one crawling, stinging thing which adds up to the total horror that Macbeth feels. Therefore, the "plot" of the nightmare ought to be considered not in terms of its literal happenings and facts, but in terms of the total emotional pattern which these events create. It is in the total form, or its general shape, that the dream becomes a metaphor. "But," one may ask, "why does such a dream disturb us so greatly?"

Let us imagine a situation which the nightmare might mirror. Suppose that a man is very ambitious; at the least he feels he must have considerable comfort and security, and at the most he wants to be president of his company; therein lie his desires. But in his company are several men whose training, ability, and company status threaten even the present security which the man enjoys. Danger and difficulty are everywhere. True, he has managed to work his way through to an assistant foremanship (the barbed wire fence), but to rise to the top of the company (the cliff) seems impossible. Yet, our sketch of the man's real-life problem is a very selective one. What about the entire picture? In addition to his potential enemies, he has numerous friends; notice also that countless peripheral dangers surround him. He drives to the factory on a dangerous highway. In the plant he is always in genuine danger of tractors, overhead cranes, and the like. If he comes home late he risks the anger of his wife and may get a cold meal. All week long his mind is occupied with the serious and not-so-serious problems connected with his job. He cannot bear to dwell on the hopelessness of professional advancement, nor can he ignore the hundreds of other problems which are with him daily. In his sleep, the situation is quite different. The most vital fears which he feels about his job are presented to him in the form of a dream. He succeeds in getting past one obstacle only to find himself clutching the rim of a precipice in agony—in short, his dream experience is emotionally the essence of his job problem. Most interestingly, the nightmare has evoked an emotional pattern which is perhaps more vivid than what he feels (or allows himself to feel) when face to face with the problem. Against his will, apparently, he has emotionally realized his problem. One may argue that this kind of realization has done him no discernible good, but this does not alter the fact that in spite of his inclinations to the contrary, he has communicated with himself in a most powerful way.

When the dreamer tried to discover what his dream meant, he treated this analysis first as a question of literal or denotative reference. Hence he thought he had discovered something important when he recalled where he had actually seen such a fence and such a type of stone as the dream depicted. But this approach was not satisfactory. Once the dreamer switched to looking at the dream as a metaphor, he had an easier time accounting for factors which had seemed mysterious or irrational when approached literally.

The essential meaning of a play also seems mysterious or irrational: ". . . that 'meaning' which alone will explain the form of the play is something . . . akin to the 'meaning' of a Rembrandt or of a Beethoven sonata." This deeper, elusive meaning in plays, which generations of critics have stressed, can be approached by realizing that a play creates its meaning for the audience in a manner very like the operation of the dream in the example. It is the overall pattern of the dream that has meaning; in the same way, the overall pattern of the play has meaning.

The pattern of the dream is the essence of the dreamer's reaction to a complex of experiences. This pattern is an idea. In the same way, the form of a dramatic action is an idea, and this pattern is the essence of the playwright's reaction to a complex of experiences. Like the meaning of the dream, the meaning of the play is a metaphorical image. No matter how philosophical, logical, or real most plays seem, their reality, logic, or philosophy are parts of a larger meaning—a meaning which orders and patterns all these parts and may therefore be called a commanding image.

This commanding image is the essence of the playwright's communication. This essence, like the meaning of the dream, is a realization, a concept, a felt significance—expressed through the impact of the total form.

Through understanding how a play means, it is now possible to formulate a new definition of a play, a definition which encompasses all drama from the most ancient to the latest avant-garde experiments:

A play is an image of human life created in the minds of an audience by the enactment of a pattern of events.

	In the Nightmare of Climbing	*In the Tragedy of Oedipus*
The *total effect* is	a particular realization of *terror*	a particular realization of *the tragic*
The *literal action* is	a climb to a destination	a search for an identity
The *literal content* is	a fence a mountain the person involved	a plague an unsolved murder a threatening prophesy the characters involved

But Does Literal Action + Literal Content = Total Effect?

Does	fence + mountain + person + climb	Does	plague + unsolved murder + prophesy + characters + search
	= a realization of terror?		= a realization of the tragic?

Apparently Not, for:	A simple total of its physical facts and events is not enough to account for the degree of terror felt during the dream	The events and physical facts used in the tragedy of Oedipus *might* add up to soap opera

Thus,
the Meaning — *of the Nightmare* — *of the Tragedy*

Is Not to Be Found in the Literal Elements.

The meaning of the dream is found in the image of the dreamer's tensions which his dream thrusts upon him, in the nonlogical but nonetheless real knowledge-of-self which is the dream.

The meaning of the play is found in what we have called the commanding image, which has been described in many ways:

As the playwright's	*As the play's*
Insight	**Action**
Intuition	**Basic line**
Vision	**Basic action**
Observation	**Basic rhythm**
Perception	**Core**
Concept	**Spine**
Idea	**Tone**
Attitude	**Major value**
Intent	**Dominant emotion**
	Dynamic spirit
	Over and above
	Superobjective
	Atmosphere
	Soul
	Essence
	Point of view

and as the interpreter's "sense of the whole."

Which is to say that the meaning of the play is to be found in that which causes the physical facts and events to become an image; in that which selects the content, orders the action, and, in fact, *is* the whole.

How does a play mean? *The essential meaning of a play is expressed through the impact of its form.*

Despite the similarity, plays are in important ways unlike dreams:

In the dream, image making is purely intuitive	*No one deliberately creates a dream—*	In the play, image making is both intuitive and conscious
	and plays are not "dreamed up"	
In the dream, literal content is rarely worth studying in and for itself		In the play, literal content is usually worth studying in and for itself
In the dream, the author communicates with himself	*Dreams are private;* *art is public*	In the play, the author communicates with an audience
In the dream, only the dreamer can judge the effectiveness of the communication		In the play, (which, like all works of art, is social) the effectiveness can be examined and discussed
	We do not expect dreams to be masterpieces	

In sum, then, the commanding image is the essential meaning of the play, which, like the meaning of any work of art, is expressed through the impact of its total form.

The fundamental aim of interpretation is to grasp the commanding image, to sense the total form as the author felt it. Thus, the interpretation of a play is a problem like the playwright's—discovering the pattern or form of action that embodies the intended meaning.

THE NATURE OF THE MEDIUM AS PART OF THE PLAY'S MEANING

But in the making of art, the commanding image—the idea —and the medium in which it is formed are separable only in theory; in actual fact they are a single thought. A sculptor's "idea" is not a vague something that he later decides to form in marble, in glass, welded steel rods, or mahogany. The sculptor thinks thoughts in wood, wire, glass, or stone.

4

Michelangelo's unfinished "Atlas":

Non ha l'Ottimo artista alcun concetto,
Ch'un marmor solo in se non circonscriva
Col suo soverchio; e solo a quello arriva
La man che ubbidisce all' intelleto—

(From a poem by Michelangelo)

No concept does the supreme artist have
That the marble itself does not enclose in its excess stone;
And only to that marble-held idea comes
The hand obedient to the artist's mind.[5]

In the same way, the playwright must think in his medium, and his images are limited by the possibilities inherent in it.

The form of the play is an idea conceived by the playwright in terms of:

A specific theatre building.

6

7

A particular audience.

A particular acting style.

8

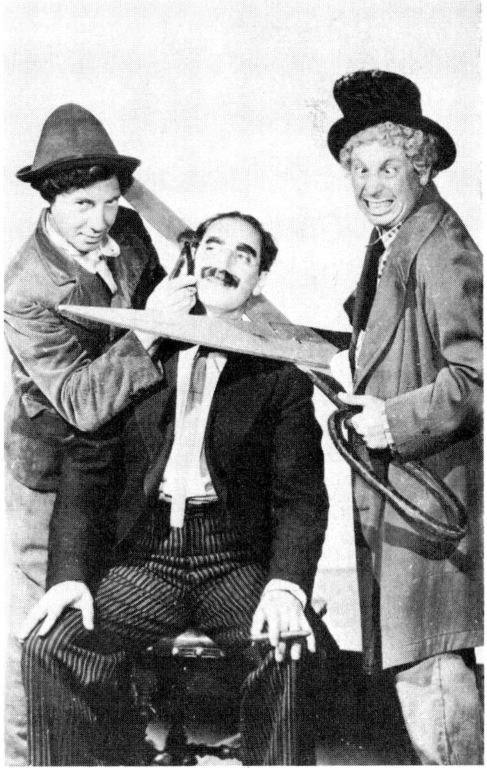

9

And often even specific actors.

Shakespeare wrote *Hamlet* with the qualities of Richard Burbage in mind.

This has been used to explain the Queen's line, "He's fat, and scant of breath." More important as a clue to the author's image is the fact that Burbage's reputation as the greatest actor of his time rested on his performances of such parts as Hieronimo, Richard III, Lear, and Othello—roles not characterized by thought-sick, silent-suffering indecision.

In *Death of a Salesman,* the time and place of the action frequently shift with the smoothness and rapidity of thought, with these changes often taking place in the mind of Willy Loman.

In deciding why the play took on this particular rhythmic pattern, it is important to realize that Arthur Miller's concept of theatre included the cinematic flow from one scene to another made possible by modern lighting control. In preparing a production of this play, the "casting" of the lighting man—who should be an artist sensitive to the moods and rhythms of the performance—becomes almost as important as the selection of some of the actors.

The audience for which Congreve wrote was made up of his personal acquaintances, members of a self-and-class-conscious coterie. For this actor-audience clique, he composed brilliant conversation to be played among them in the candle-lit coziness of their salon theatre.

Which suggests that, in addition to the customary polish and precision of delivery, personal charm and an intimate rapport with the audience are key factors in the acting style appropriate for Restoration comedy. Snobbish affectation that makes an audience feel inferior to the actors can turn production of these plays into chilly museum pieces.

As he composed them, Sophocles "heard" his speeches projected through a mask into a space like a football stadium.

"In the theatre where Sophocles performed, an actor standing before the scene house was twenty yards from the first row of spectators and one-hundred yards from the last row. A six-foot actor looked three and one-half inches high to the front row and three-quarters of an inch high to the last row."[10] *Which means that Sophocles' concept of this play simply could not include those small symptoms of behavior which—seen and heard at close range—create the surface appearances so necessary to modern psychological realism.*

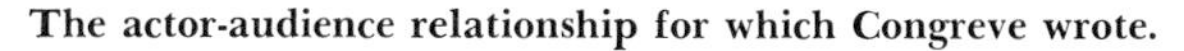

The actor-audience relationship for which Congreve wrote.

11

A modern production of a Greek tragedy in the ancient theatre of Epidauros.

The Idea of Man

But the playwright's medium involves more than his theatre and its actors. The large, simple, virile effects demanded by Sophocles were only in part due to the theatrical context in which his plays were performed; these effects were also consistent with the Periclean idea of man, an image quite different from the twentieth-century man's view of himself:

Statue: Fifth century B.C.

Numberless are the world's wonders, but none
More wonderful than man; the stormgrey sea
Yields to his prows, the huge crests bear him high;
Earth, holy and inexhaustible, is graven
With shining furrows where his plows have gone
Year after year, the timeless labour of stallions.

. . . .

Words, also, and thought as rapid as air,
He fashions to his good use; statecraft is his,
And his the skill that deflects the arrows of snow,
The spears of winter rain: from every wind
He has made himself secure—from all but one:
In the late wind of death he cannot stand.

Sophocles, 442 B.C.[14]

Statue: Twentieth century A.D.

People are humble and frightened and guilty at heart, all of us, no matter how desperately we may try to appear otherwise. We have very little conviction of our essential dignity nor even of our essential decency, and consequently we are more interested in characters on the stage who share our hidden shames and fears, and we want the plays about us to say "I understand you. You and I are brothers, the deal is rugged but let's face and fight it together."

It is not the essential dignity but the essential ambiguity of man that I think needs to be stated.

Tennessee Williams, 1960 A.D.[15]

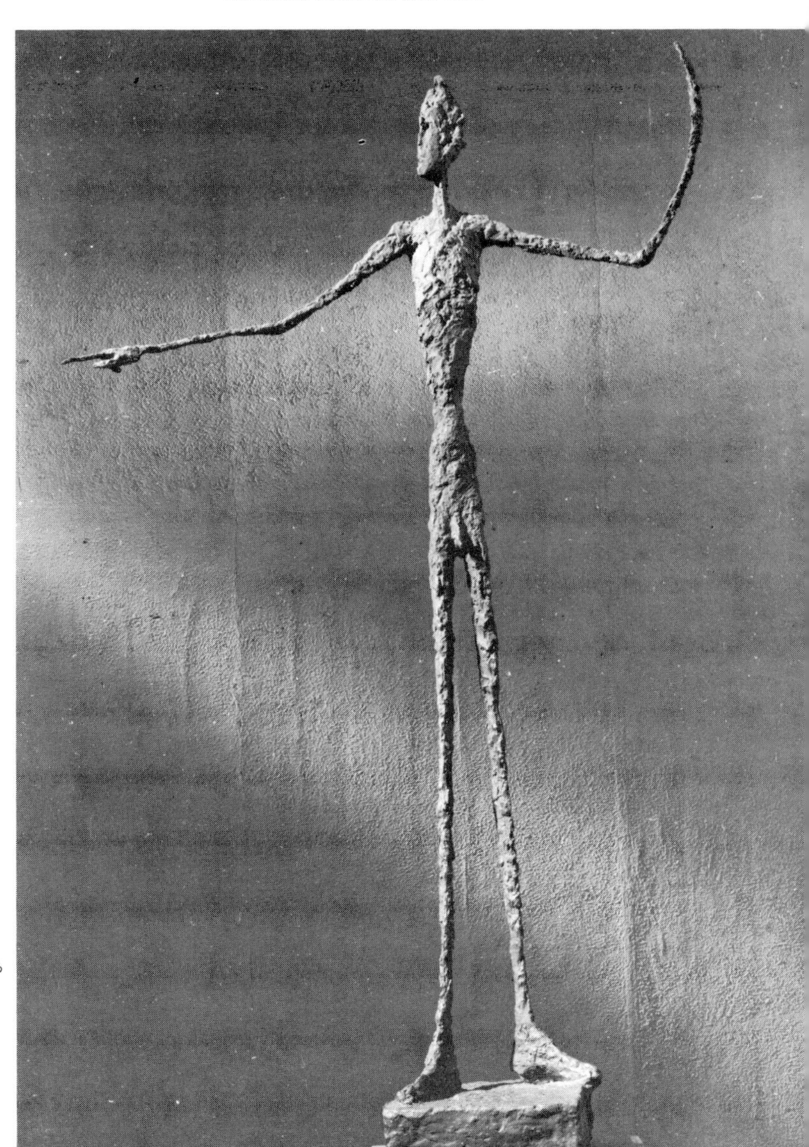

Periclean sculpture and drama express one and the same image of man; the same can be said of twentieth-century sculpture and the image of man described by one of our leading playwrights. But the glaring contrast between these two images clearly shows why the performance style created for the kind of man one finds in Gorki, Chekhov, and Williams will not fit the idea of man found in the plays of Sophocles. A modern realistic character is one who has psychological dimension of such elaborate and subtle detail that he can be recognized in clinical terms. Our actors today have become marvelously skilled in portraying such detail, so it is no wonder that we are prone to performing Oedipus the King as if he were such a man. And it is no wonder that we fail to see the marvelous irony in portraying him as if he had some kind of complex. The Oedipus of the script has no complex. The syndrome is missing: the script ignores the telltale traces which betray a life of tensions and anxieties; the subtle evidences of neurotic disturbance, the nervous starts, hesitancies, distracted mutterings, and glances that are made so revealing by our talented modern actor-psychologists—these are not to be found in the play. Certainly Oedipus has problems—big ones—but he is not a man made up of symptoms. In short, he is Sophocles' man—"none more wonderful"—not Williams's man, "humble and frightened and guilty at heart." The fall of Sophocles' Oedipus is all the more terrible because of his awesome stature. To squeeze him into the smaller forms of modern realism is to fail to re-create the commanding image of this play, for the vision of man and of his world held in common by a playwright and his audience is an essential part of the medium out of which the author's commanding images are formed.

Facts

It has been heavily stressed that the essential meaning, the commanding image, of a play cannot be found by studying it in a literal fashion. However, this should not be taken to mean that the literal contents of a play are unimportant —in fact, the opposite is true. Flights of aesthetic inspiration based on scant knowledge of what the play is about have resulted in productions even more objectionable than those dragged to earth by excessive literalism, especially in recent years, as the pictures of *Macbeth* and *Hamlet* productions have shown.

The commanding image is composed of emotional reactions to concrete things; these reactions cannot occur in the interpreter unless the literal contents are fully understood. He must understand the facts and events as the author's audience understood them, or the image will not emerge. It is in this sense that the audience is part of the playwright's medium. The interpreter must understand what the play is about and its relation to the playwright's world—its culture, society, and current events.

For example, current events are crucial to the understanding of Euripides' *The Trojan Women.* Often called a "pacifist" play, its historic context shows that "pacifist" is too simple a description. Euripides' attitude toward the war with Sparta changed from enthusiastic support when he believed in the Athenian cause to disillusionment when Athens grew imperialistic. Disillusion turned to horror when the Athenians wantonly massacred the men and enslaved the women of the tiny neutralist island of Melos in 416 B.C. *The Trojan Women,* performed the next year, reenacts this event in a mythical setting. The play is a cry of horror at what the Athenians, the most civilized community of the ancient world, had come to:

> **Around the altars they slaughtered us.**
> **Within their beds lay headless men,**
> **Young men cut down in their prime.**
> **This was the triumph-crown of Greece.**

Though the agony of the war victims is used to make the event horrible, the event depicted is not war in general; the event—what the play is about—is an atrocity committed by the Greeks. The tragedy is not the historic fall of Troy, but the contemporary moral fall of the Athenians. This means that, in production, one would not cut the prologue, as some producers have, for the prologue, in which the Gods resolve to punish the Greeks for their crimes, emphasizes the fate of Athens rather than the fate of the women of Troy.

The canonization of Joan of Arc in 1920 is a vital part of the context in which Shaw wrote *Saint Joan.* The Epilogue, in which a Gentleman from 1920 joins the fifteenth-century characters to announce the canonization, has been criticized as "anticlimactic, redundant, a clownish trick." Shaw, maintaining that Joan's canonization was an event more important than her burning, insisted that the Epilogue must stand. In this scene everyone, including the man from 1920, recoils in horror from the idea that Joan might return to earth; this is essential to Shaw's ironic observation that we feel safer with saints that are dead. If the Epilogue seems out of place, it may be because the rest of the play has been misinterpreted. It is the interpreter's task to make his audience see that the scene is an integral part of Shaw's commanding image, and that though the play's story is set in the fifteenth century, its meaning is aimed at the twentieth.

But mastery of the facts and events can also mean knowing when they are *not* important. Critics under the impression that Arthur Miller is a left-of-center social critic have been misled into looking at *Death of a Salesman* as a simple condemnation of the capitalist system. As such, they find the play fuzzy in its message and not at all satisfactory. However, a close reading of the play shows no sign of a blanket condemnation of any economic system. Willy Loman's mistaken vision of his world is not universally shared by other characters in the play, some of whom have succeeded in the very same environment. What the play essentially shows is the torment of a misguided individual. Its lesser impact in England, where the Lomans and their ideals are apparently not so numerous as in America, underlines the fact that it is not primarily a criticism of an economic system but rather a portrayal of a man whose life has been built upon some unfortunate American cultural myths about success.

Another example of the artistic value of facts and events is offered by Paul Muni whose dedication to detailed research is well known. His statement illustrates an artist's use of literal research—not to provide facts for logical explanations of meaning, but to furnish the interpreter's mind with the content out of which an image can be formed:

> *Muni:* **When I was working on *The Story of Louis Pasteur*, I read most everything . . . I could lay my hands on that had to do with Pasteur, with Lister, with his contemporaries. . . . I read everything. . . . I mean, a fellow like Ehrlich, who had no connection with Pasteur, . . . but he also dealt in the same field. I**

read up everything I could on Ehrlich and others like that. . . .

Interviewer: **Do you study photographs, too?**

Muni: **I study photographs, but not as much.**

Interviewer: **What does all this do for you?**

Muni: **I don't know. I don't pretend to—I don't want to know. . . . It's one of those things. You become saturated with some kind of psychological images, if you can use that term at all. It's one of those things that you do not—you do not methodically work out. It's one of those things you throw yourself into, a kind of, if you can call it that, miasmic thing that is just a conglomerate business, and you just pick out whatever instinctively seems to fit into the pattern of what you—what you're looking for.**[17]

This careful research into literal context, which is one of the reasons Muni insists on having his scripts months in advance, equips him to "pick out whatever instinctively seems to fit into the pattern," to get the "feel" of a character or play—to form the commanding image.

In sum, then, the answer to the question "How does a play mean?" is twofold. The play's fundamental meaning—the thing which makes its pattern of human action *art* and not history, philosophy, or psychology—is a metaphorical communication of experience, an "idea" of feelings, a meaningful form. But this form is shaped out of the raw materials of concrete reality: the playwright's concept of acting, the actors he knows, the theatre he works in, and his sense of his audience—a whole complex of manners, mores, tastes, and attitudes which includes such things as history, philosophy, and psychology. The impact of all these factors significantly affects the form in which the playwright is able to conceive a dramatic idea—they are all part of the nature of the playwright's medium, and so must be studied to fully comprehend the author's intended meaning and must be dealt with in creating a production to express it.

THE PROBLEM OF TRANSLATION

Does the necessity of dealing with the playwright's theatre and his sense of his audience mean that, in the production of classics for example, the playwright's intent is best expressed by a facsimile of the original production? Some producers seem to think so—the enthusiasm for Globe theatres involves the idea that the truest interpretations of Shakespeare are archeologically correct reproductions of Elizabethan staging.

These Globe reconstructions follow the principle of exhibiting art objects in the style and surroundings of their period, a most helpful educational device also employed by leading art museums. Seriously and consistently applied, this facsimile approach deals with the playwright's concept of acting, his theatre, and also with his sense of his audience and their world.

But—does a modern audience see Shakespeare's stage as his audience saw it? To Shakespeare's audience, this stage was the familiar scaffold on which all plays were acted, so their attention was focused on the actors. But to a modern audience this stage is scenery, interesting in itself as an archeological attraction; the audience's attention may wander to the set and to the period manners—to acting conventions which may at times become more a part of this unusual scenic decoration than of the meaning of the play.

However, no one really tries to duplicate the actual conditions of the Elizabethan performances, to carry the idea to its logical end; none of the advocates of Globe staging have consistently:

Staged the plays without cutting and modifying the texts

Performed in the afternoon sun, or indoors, without resorting to modern lighting control emphasizing special areas

Kept as much light on the audience as on the actors

Made a large part of their audience stand around the stage or had their actors read the lines in Elizabethan accents

Thus, all revivals of period plays differ from the original staging, and for the same crucial reason: some deviation from absolute archeology is necessary, for although the original audience is part of the medium in which the playwright's image was formed, there is no way of duplicating in the modern audience the minds of the original audience —their mental picture of the stage, of dramatic art, of the world in which they lived.

The task of the interpreter, then, must be to bring the commanding image to the audience. He does this by contributing his sense of his own audience to the medium in which the idea is conveyed.

Thus, the good interpreter (director, actor, or designer) has studied the playwright's sense of his audience; he has his own sense of his own audience; and he expresses one in terms of the other. In this sense, all play production is a problem in translation.

For translation is not only a problem for producers of classics or of foreign-language plays. Many modern productions, even when there is no language barrier, suffer in being moved from one audience to another. A Broadway hit may fail west of the Hudson, while a play that quickly closed in New York may have a long and prosperous life in the nation's community theatres. London hits transported to Broadway may fail, as many have, or be transformed by audience reactions alone into what is, in effect, a different play, as Tyrone Guthrie testifies about *The Matchmaker*:

> **The really disconcerting thing was to find what a completely different play the American audience made it seem. . . . In the face of audience reaction throughout a four-week tryout the whole performance became sharper, harder, tougher with—in my opinion—considerable loss of charm. . . . Mr. Merrick was alarmed and declared with some heat that this was not the play he had bought in London. Thornton Wilder was infected with the same fever. He saw a matinee in which every line was spoken, every bit of business performed, as exactly and meticulously as it had been for more than a year by an experienced and well-disposed company. He and Merrick fell upon me as if I were a fraudulent dogbreeder who had sold them a mongrel with a forged pedigree.**[18]

Thus, in the terms used so far, a good production of any play might be defined as a production which expresses the playwright's commanding image—an image which contains his concepts of acting, the theatre, his audience, and world-view—in terms of a particular audience.

Always follow the natural paths of creation, the growth of forms and their functions. That is the best way to learn. Perhaps you may through nature arrive at the point where you can create on your own. Then one day you yourself will be a part of nature; you will be able to create as she does.

PAUL KLEE[1]

PART TWO: **The Process of Interpretation**

LORNA: Success and fame! Or just a lousy living. You're lucky you won't have to worry about those things. . . .
JOE: Won't I?
LORNA: Unless Tom Moody's a liar.
JOE: You like him, don't you?
LORNA: [*After a pause*] I like him.
JOE: I like how you dress. The girls look nice in the summer time. Did you ever stand at the Fifth Avenue Library and watch those girls go by?
LORNA: No, I never did. [*Switching the subject*] That's the carousel, that music. Did you ever ride on one of those?
JOE: That's for kids.
LORNA: Weren't you ever a kid, for God's sake?
JOE: Not a happy kid.
LORNA: Why?
JOE: Well, I always felt different. Even my name was special—Bonaparte—and my eyes . . .
LORNA: I wouldn't have taken that too serious. . . .
[*There is a silent pause. Joe looks straight ahead*]
JOE: Gee, all those cars . . .
LORNA: Lots of horses trot around here. The rich know how to live. You'll be rich. . . .
JOE: My brother Frank is an organizer for the C.I.O.
LORNA: What's that?
JOE: If you worked in a factory you'd know. Did you ever work?
LORNA: [*With a smile*] No, when I came out of the cocoon I was a butterfly and butterflies don't work.
JOE: All those cars . . . whizz, whizz. [*Now turning less casual*] Where's Mr. Moody tonight?
LORNA: He goes up to see his kid on Tuesday
LORNA: Tokio says you're going far in the fighting game.
JOE: Music means more to me. May I tell you something?
LORNA: Of course.
JOE: If you laugh I'll never speak to you again.
LORNA: I'm not the laughing type.
JOE: With music I'm never alone when I'm alone—Playing music . . . that's like saying, "I am man. I belong here. How do you do, World—good evening!" When I play music nothing is closed to me. I'm not afraid of people and what they say. There's no war in music. It's not like the streets. Does this sound funny?
LORNA: No.
JOE: But when you leave your room . . . down in the street . . . it's war. Music can't help me there. Understand?
LORNA: Yes.
JOE: People have hurt my feelings for years. I never forget. You can't get even with people by playing the fiddle. If music shot bullets I'd like it better—artists and people like that are freaks today. The world moves fast and they sit around like forgotten dopes.

Interpretation, as has been said, is to a great extent the reconstruction or re-creation of the creative process through which the playwright has gone. It seems only reasonable then for the interpreter to follow whatever processes are natural to the playwright's way of creating his play.

The matter of instinct or intuition must be taken into account as something natural to any artist's creativity, and, indeed, producing the play by instinct or inspiration may at times communicate the playwright's idea even though the interpreters have never consciously identified it. In such cases, it may be said that inspiration = intuitive grasp of the commanding image.

But, of course, a sudden flash of enthusiasm for a highly original but wrong idea is often mistaken for inspiration, and even true inspiration is not a way of working, not something that can be depended upon and deliberately brought into play. Most artists have enough craftsmanship to keep their creative activity going between the unpredictable bursts of insight and illumination, and the interpreter, whether or not he believes in "systems," develops a set of skills with which to work.

The theory of theatrical meaning just presented leads to a useful way of working, one that follows "the natural paths of creation."

THREE BASIC PROBLEMS

In terms of this idea of what theatrical art is and how it works, it is possible to organize the process of interpretation into three basic problems: Since artistic meaning is metaphorical, one key question becomes—"What is the play like?" Since the medium in which the playwright forms his metaphor includes literal content and its significance to the audience, a second key question becomes—"What is the play about?" Since the medium in which the playwright forms his metaphor includes his idea of theatre, a third key question becomes—"What is the play's theatrical context?" If the analysis is successful, the answers to all three of these questions will be embodied in the production which emerges.

To find the meaning of a play by asking what it is about and by examining its theatrical context is, of course, nothing new. Literal methods of analysis have been handled so frequently that there is no need for elaboration here. The same is true of techniques for analyzing play construction—for examining such matters as the inciting incident, exposition, complication, climax, and denouement that make up plot structure—the scenes, motivational units, and beats of which the performance is built, and the motivations, actions, and spines basic to each characterization. All these matters, important to any intelligent production of a play, have been discussed many times. But the figurative analysis of theatrical meaning is another matter. It is this aspect of artistic meaning which has been understood the least, and so how one goes about answering "What is the play like?" must be described in full. However, before delving into the question of figurative analysis, an indication of what the other questions imply seems in order. The following list is intended to serve as a suggestive reminder of the approaches followed in literal analysis.

What Is the Play's Theatrical Context?

Evidence from the playscript and evidence from other sources

is used to answer questions about the playwright's stage:

How does the script reveal the relationship between the form of the play and the form of the theatre through indications of:

- Levels and acting areas
- Scenic conventions
- Mechanical devices, etc.?

What information about the physical form and equipment of the theatre throws light on the form of the play?

and to answer questions about the playwright's players:

What acting conventions are assumed in the script:

- Illusion of ordinary conversation
- Asides
- Soliloquies
- Tirades?

What information about the performers' practices illuminates the content of the script?

What relationship between performance and audience does the script imply? Is the acting to be:

- Character to character (realistic illusion)
- Character to audience (open stage, classical)
- Actor to audience (*commedia dell'arte*, vaudeville, musical revue)?

Through what particular acting conventions did the audience expect to see the play?

What Is the Play About?

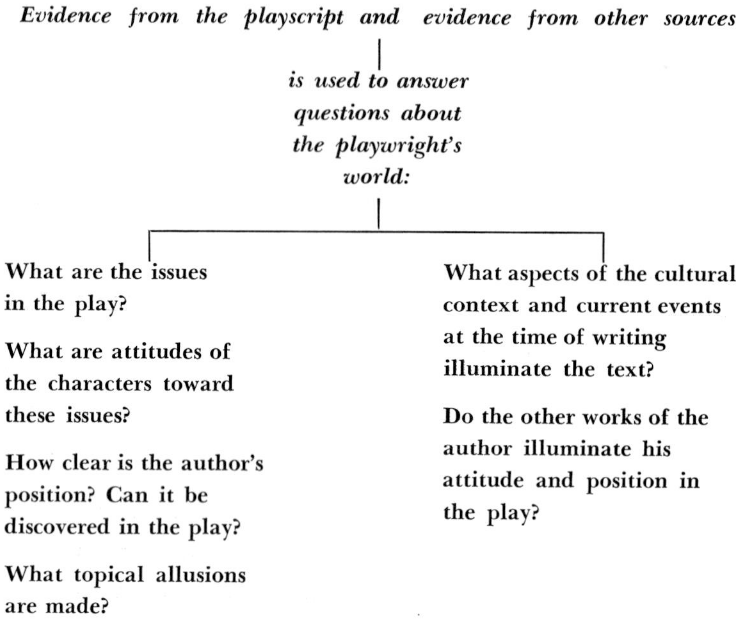

Evidence from the playscript and evidence from other sources

is used to answer questions about the playwright's world:

What are the issues in the play?

What are attitudes of the characters toward these issues?

How clear is the author's position? Can it be discovered in the play?

What topical allusions are made?

What aspects of the cultural context and current events at the time of writing illuminate the text?

Do the other works of the author illuminate his attitude and position in the play?

These questions dealing with theatrical context and factual data serve very well in understanding literal meaning, but are no direct help in clarifying that elusive "meaning which alone will explain the form of the play." What follows is an extended discussion of techniques and devices which have been or could be used to grasp this elusive meaning.

What Is the Play Like?

> Poetical abstractions are beautiful and new, not because the portions of which they are composed had no previous existence in the mind of man or in nature, but because

> **the whole produced by their combination has some intelligible and beautiful *analogy* with those sources of emotion and thought. . . .**
>
> *Percy Bysshe Shelley*[2]

Since the nature of theatrical meaning is metaphorical —as is all artistic meaning—the natural way for the interpreter to search for the figurative meaning of the play is through analytical techniques which follow the same operating principle as metaphor. Metaphor operates by association. The play's commanding image must be sought through associational techniques.

Through these associational techniques the interpreter tries to answer the key question: "What is the play like?" Simply stated, the answer or answers to this question intensify the interpreter's sense of the play and help him to realize, by analogy to other experiences, that idea of experience which is the commanding image of the play. The sources of analogous experience can be as varied as life itself. The more varied the interpreter's experiences, the more potential analogies he has for interpreting the play.

The time available for most production is inadequate for anything more than hurried research and analysis. This means that the information needed for the literal analysis of the play, and the experiences necessary for the associational analysis of the play's form, must have been acquired before work begins on any particular production. Therefore, it must be assumed that a good theatre artist is a person with a substantial education—formal or otherwise—that he is widely experienced, and that his interest keeps him continually reading and thinking in a wide variety of subjects and areas.

READING THE PLAY

The first reading of the play, as many writers have pointed out, is a most important one to the interpreter, for his unstudied first impressions may come quite close to the play's intended meaning. Some discussion of the first reading is therefore in order.

Since the first reading is to get a sense of the shape of the whole, to feel the effect of it as a performance, the play should be read at a single sitting so that it moves uninterrupted through time. During this time, what happens (if one is the ideally equipped stage director of Gordon Craig's imagination) is that ". . . the entire colour, tone, movement and rhythm that the work must assume comes clearly before him." Though many would object that it might take more than one reading to come to such a satisfyingly right impression, Craig's next statement has provoked no opposition and has become a commonplace admonition in modern production theory:

> **As for the stage directions, descriptions of the scenes, etc., with which the author may interlard his copy, these are not to be considered by him [the interpreter], for if he is master of his craft he can learn nothing from them.**
>
> ***On the Art of the Theatre, 1911***[3]

Stage Directions

Craig goes on to assert that the playwright, in daring to write stage directions, "poaches" on the stage director's preserves, and equates this with an actor adding "gags" to the script. Craig assumes that the playwright knows little or nothing about staging, which makes his notes useless. Some of Craig's followers go further and would have the interpreter strip the play of everything except the dialogue, for they feel that the author's stage directions may actually interfere with the free play of the interpreter's imagination, creating "sterile first impressions" that cannot later be dislodged.

Contrary to these widely held views, a more logical position would be that the advantage of having all possible clues to the playwright's intended meaning far outweighs the possible disadvantage of reading a script in which the author has inadequately visualized the production. Therefore the interpreter should read everything the playwright has written, including all stage directions, character descriptions, ideas for costumes and settings, and anything else the author cares to describe. Removing the stage directions before reading shows a lack of confidence, not only in the author, but in the interpreter's own strength of imagination. If the interpreter reads stage directions as the playwright's attempts to describe effects desired rather than as exact blueprints of staging, he may find in them valuable aids to his understanding of the play. For example,

> **The Wingfield apartment is in the rear of the building, one of those vast, hive-like conglomerations of cellular living-units . . . burning with the slow . . . fires of human desperation. The fire escape is included in the set.**
>
> ***Williams, The Glass Menagerie***

The words "hive-like," "cellular," and "burning" all contribute to the image of the apartment as part of a crowded hell from which the hero, entering and leaving by means of the fire escape, finally escapes.

And in *Blood Wedding,* Lorca gives this stage direction for Act I, scene 3:

> **Interior of the cave where the Bride lives. At the back is a cross of rose colored flowers. Around the walls which are of white, hard material, are round fans, blue jars and little mirrors.**

The fact, nowhere else mentioned, that the room is in a cave and that the walls are white and hard, coupled with the scattered bits of color and decoration, leads to the image of a parched, tomblike chalk prison, pitifully decorated by its female inmates—a scenic image admirably suited to the content of the scene and of the play as a whole.

Titles and Names

The first reading of the play should also include careful attention to the play's title and to the character names—a more often used than discussed set of clues to the author's intentions. Sometimes the playwright chooses a name for its tone color and suggestive qualities, but often he constructs names which not only have an evocative value, but contain factual information as well. Thus the use of titles and names as clues straddles literal analysis and associational analysis, with a foot in each camp.

Enid Bagnold has offered an interesting group of names that are both suggestive and carry concrete data about the play and its characters.

Miss Bagnold's title, *The Chalk Garden,* is, in a sense, the commanding image of her play, which (allegorically) views England as a sterile soil, barren of opportunity for its youth, no longer Shakespeare's "teeming womb of royal kings." England is both the sterile garden of the title and the eccentric grandmother figure who, in the play, tries to cultivate it. In choosing names for her characters, the playwright has taken great care to make every name indicative of both the individual and his place in the scheme of the play. Thus Mrs. St. Maugham, the name of the grandmother, suggests in its musical and aristocratic sound the decaying old order, "the Establishment"; the daughter and granddaughter of this ancient "gardener" have the names of traditionally symbolic plants—Olive and Laurel—which are descriptive of their positions in the play: Olive, the mother, comes to offer peace and to claim her daughter Laurel, who is the prize that motivates the play's conflict. The mysterious, serious woman who comes as Laurel's governess has the gay, seemingly inappropriate name Madrigal. In one definition, "madrigal" means "an invented song"—and indeed, the name turns out to be an alias, but it is appropriate to another level, for it is Madrigal who is instrumental in bringing some semblance of harmony to the household and the garden. Maitland, the ex-convict manservant who avidly reads *Notable Trials,* bears the name of a famous nineteenth century British jurist and historian —and so it goes.

The playwright does not draw the audience's attention to these names, and it would be a mistake for the interpreter to treat the naming pattern more seriously than the author has, for the basic merit of the play certainly does not depend on the playfully cunning scheme of its names. However, the script as a whole is organized by an allegorical idea; the names are meticulously, but unobtrusively, a part of this structure, and therefore the interpreter who neglects to investigate the names will have missed some helpful clues to the author's intent.

The possible range from literal description to poetic imagery is illustrated further in the following play titles:

Literal

↑

Through his title, *The Way of the World,* Congreve named his purpose—a commentary on the manners and mores of his society.

Ibsen named *Hedda Gabler* after the central character of the play, a common practice; but the uncommon fact that he used Mrs. Tesman's maiden name is descriptively significant.

The title of Miller's *The Crucible* is at once an image and a description of the play—for the play's action is the fiery process in which the protagonist finds his morality.

Sarte's *No Exit* and Kingsley's *Dead End* borrow their titles from common urban signs, and both sum up the position in which the characters find themselves.

***Summer and Smoke* evokes the sense of repressed, smouldering heat and suggests the conflict between flesh and spirit basic to Williams's play.**

↓

Metaphorical

Williams's character naming also displays a range from description to suggestion, but leans toward the latter. Thus the central character in *Summer and Smoke* is called Alma, and a point is made in the dialogue that her name is Spanish for "soul"—a case of rather literal naming, though the soft sound of the word connotes her character. On the other hand, Blanche Dubois and Stanley Kowalski are chiefly associational in their impact. Kowalski suggests the brute force of the football field, the stevedore, the mill hand. In the context of the Old South, the name also suggests a foreign invader, a recurring theme in Williams's plays. Blanche DuBois carries a feeling of antebellum elegance and delicacy; translated, it indicates something of Williams's attitude toward the character: *blanche*—white, virginal, pure; *du bois*—of the wood, hence a creature from some elegant woodland park thrust into an urban slum ironically named "Elysian Fields" and reached by a streetcar named "Desire." Though the place names may actually exist in New Orleans, their selection is poetic rather than literal.

Further Readings of the Play

In getting the feeling of what the play is like, further study of the script can be used to sharpen one's sense of particular scenes, characters, and other fragmentary units of the work.

Ultimately, it is a keen and consistent sense of the whole that one hopes to get, but it is time to point out that, for more than one reason, to begin the process with a self-conscious search for some immediately recognizable Grand Image is a mistake. The playwright himself may struggle for months, perhaps even years, with the concrete details of characterization, dialogue, plot, and so on before he is finally satisfied that the whole fabric is woven together in the right shape. Whatever the dominating "idea" of experience that gave the play its final form, it was realized in no small measure *while* the author struggled with his medium; it was not a pure, disembodied perception before any attempt was made to give it utterance. The observation made earlier that idea and medium are really one and inseparable implies this fact; the artist, as he tries to perfect a particular work, continually discovers things about his medium and its possibilities, and so his idea continually reshapes itself in terms of the medium. This is even more true in the production of a play, for the interpreter (let us say, the director) must take into account the potentialities and limitations of the other interpreters (actors, designer, technicians)—an aspect of the medium most crucial to *him* —and therefore must shape the final result accordingly.

Considering that each production adds new and unique elements to the medium, the interpreter will have to be cautious about Great Discoveries and their often doctrinaire aftereffects. And considering how the play's form or idea was probably arrived at, he can hardly expect to launch into a script armed with theories of theatrical art and immediately win the day by identifying the play's total figurative meaning—and least of all can he expect to find this meaning in a form that can be easily communicated to others.

What he can expect, however, is to find that at least some of the play will easily stage itself in his imagination in ways that he feels to be right, and he should keep in mind that in actual practice the playwright's meaning can be approached from either of two directions, or even from both at once:

From the whole to the parts	or	*from the parts to the whole*
	← →	the director may discover the whole play through directing a single scene or series of scenes
an organizing principle may be discovered which serves as a criterion for the selection and ordering of the parts	← →	the director may find his sense of the play suddenly clarified in one of the thumbnail sketches made by the designer
	← →	the actor may come across the key to his characterization in a hand prop or the look and feel of his costume

Thus, the initial readings of the script and early rehearsals may very well turn out to be a struggle with isolated problems—with the pieces rather than the whole configuration—and there is every reason to use this phase of the work to get an interpretative grip on these details through use of associational techniques. As the following illustrations show, a more concrete idea of a property, a stage movement, or a characterization may be imagined by metaphorical thinking and may in turn lead to a clearer sense of the whole.

METAPHORICAL THINKING

A clear image that captures the meaning of a key prop may also include implications for scenic treatment as well as for the function of the prop in the action.

The stage directions of *The Glass Menagerie* say, of the prop that gives the play its title, "In an old-fashioned whatnot . . . are seen scores of transparent glass animals." In the play this prop functions as a lovely, fragile hiding place in a hostile environment, a refuge in constant danger of being smashed. An analogy image can help us see that this prop is like "a miraculous ice-crystal palace—in a smouldering dump," and would imply that: (1) the whatnot itself should be pale blue or white, perhaps with glass shelves, somewhat fantastic in design and unsteady looking; (2) the area in which the menagerie stands should perhaps be lit in cool blue light while the walls of the set, together with the light of the surrounding areas, should suggest the coarse and ominous texture of a hot, faintly glowing cinder.

An image can be of great practical value in planning meaningful patterns of stage movement, as Robert Lewis testified in his book, *Method or Madness?*:

> In a play I directed called *My Heart's in the Highlands,* there was a moment when an old Shakespearean actor played a tune on a horn for the villagers, and they, in order to thank him, offered him gifts. The play was, to me, about the position of the artist in the world. That particular moment, I felt, meant that the people are nourished by art, and I had the image of a plant flowering as it is being watered. How I executed that idea on the stage was, first, to have the old man high up on the porch playing his trumpet, with the people below. As he became more and more moved he started to quiver (this was justified by the actor's very real feeling, you understand) and he appeared to be using his trumpet like a watering can. The people standing around were gradually attracted to the sound and in order to listen more comfortably, a couple of

them knelt down on one knee, a child was lifted up on somebody's shoulder (all very "true" elements, you see), and when this movement was completed, the crowd was formed roughly into the shape of a tree. Now each person also had concealed in his hand a nicely colored prop, a piece of vegetable or fruit or whatever. As they listened they slowly offered these things up to the old man. Each hand that came out, presumably from this tree, had one of these props in it. The actors were still doing something real (offering gifts), but it was gradually seeming to be a tree that was flowering. Then, as they listened to the music, they started to hum and sway, and the whole effect became like a tree swaying in the breeze. At the very end of the piece, just because I couldn't resist it, the little child on the very top held up a gaily colored chicken.

It all comes down to a matter of choice. Although what each actor did was real and could be justified, there were lots of real things that they might have done that they didn't. They behaved in a certain, controlled way. It was not necessary for the people to walk up and hand the gifts to him, for example. All those inessentials, real as they might be, were cut away so that I arrived at the image, the essence.[4]

Morris Carnovsky and Helen Hayes are among the many actors who have described associational techniques which vivify their understanding of dramatic action and characterization.

Carnovsky: When I was working on Shylock, I was haunted by the idea of a broken face, and I remember certain artistic examples of this—the man with the broken nose by Rodin, a face that Picasso did, a mask, Marc

Chagall's "The Vitebsk Rabbi," Ivan Mestrovic's "Moses." . . . But most of all I remember a certain character in my youth; he was a crazy, half-demented fellow. . . . They called him Yussel the Meshugeneh—Yussel the crazy one. He was a terribly pathetic creature, terribly pathetic. And I recall the kids used to throw things at him, and there was no way of his protecting himself. He had a broken nose and a dirty, bedraggled beard, and now and then he would turn on them and ask them, "Why do you do this? What have I done to you?" And the pathos of this poor demented creature being hounded by the kids came very sharply into my mind when I was thinking about Shylock. Now, where did it come from? I hadn't thought about him for many years. But suddenly in working on Shylock it was necessary that this image should come up out of the depths and present itself to me as if to say, "Here I am, if you want to, use me." And I did. Not necessarily to make him up that way, but there was something about the identification with that image which I certainly could use.[5]

Hayes: When I was preparing for my role of the duchess in *Time Remembered,* I had some difficulty capturing the spirit of the role, until one day in Boston, while listening to the radio, I heard some music written by Giles Farnaby for the virginal—you know, one of those sixteenth-century instruments. I listened for about half an hour, and suddenly the idea came to me. That old duchess, I told myself, is like the music, light, dainty, period, pompous, tinkling. And, poor me, I'd been playing her like a bass drum. I had one scene in *Victoria Regina* that I played like one of my poodles. Believe it or not, it was just extraordinary how that

> communicated. And this vision came across my eyes once about that scene. . . . Now that gets into those secret things I mentioned before: that if you ever said at rehearsal, "Well, I think that scene is like a poodle dog," that's the end of that—you'd never get it, you'd never capture it. It's your secret with the audience and the playwright. But, anyway, it was the scene in which Disraeli was buttering up the old queen something shamelessly, and he was just paying her these florid compliments and going on—and it was a long speech, you see, and on and on he went. I sat absolutely immobile. I didn't blink an eye. And there were times when the communication was so great—well, it wasn't very nice of me, in fact, it was naughty of me, but the audience would start to laugh, and finally break into applause in the middle of the actor's speech. But it was only that inside I was just blowing up and I knew just how it felt, because I had a poodle that used to sit, and he'd almost look intoxicated when I'd say, "Oh, Turvey, you are the most beautiful dog, Turvey, you are so beautiful, what a good animal. . . ." And I'd do this just for my own amusement, and watch this poodle become a little, just a little, intoxicated—and believe me every night for the thousand and some performances of that play, I saw that poodle.[6]

Helen Hayes' contention that some interpretative ideas must remain "secret" raises a very important point about the use of associational techniques. As the illustrations above show, one may greatly clarify his own understanding of the script through associational imagining—but what about communicating this understanding to other people? The very effective poodle metaphor was drawn from a private experience, which the actress felt was nobody's literal business but her own. And rightly so. One cannot write plays, direct, or act them self-consciously, and the embarrassment of letting people in on her poodle idea would have made her painfully self-conscious. Furthermore, the experience with "Turvey," like Carnovsky's with the pathetic "Yussel," was a personal one, which could scarcely have meant as much to anyone else, so there was every reason to keep quiet about it. On the other hand, the director can scarcely keep quiet about all of his ideas concerning the playwright's intended meaning; if he uses it with a balanced sense of what is likely to embarrass, what is too uniquely personal to be effective, and what might communicate his insights to his cast and crews, a director can fruitfully employ emotional analogy to achieve the results he wants. For example, the actors under Robert Lewis's direction would probably have given believably appreciative reactions in any case, but without the flowering tree image there is considerable doubt that their individual responses would have followed any pattern consistent enough to create the more powerful feeling that a community had been made to grow and bloom by music.

What the issue comes down to is this: though the image might lead a sensitive designer or director to rather specific literal requirements of color, shape, and style for the title prop in *The Glass Menagerie,* any intelligent interpreter will realize that to add to the prop list a request for a "whatnot like a miraculous ice-crystal palace" will get only a well-deserved hoot of derision from the property man.

The examples above also suggest that associational analysis draws on any and every kind of experience: animals, people, places, events—the variety is imponderably vast. But certain kinds of experience are naturally more analogous to the dynamics of theatrical art than others and therefore more productive of effective associations. The pages that follow present examples of these categories of experience and the theatrical uses that have been or could be made of them.

ANALOGIES TO ENTERTAINMENT FORMS

Entertainment

In its other theatrical forms entertainment provides close-knit analogies which can be made with comparative ease. For example, the Yale University production of Plautus' *The Merchant* translated the play in terms of a Gay Nineties vaudeville show by an ancient Roman gag-writer, and Donald Oenslager's design for the set is a Gay Nineties act drop painted by a Pompeian muralist:

7

Similarly, E. E. Cummings' *him* uses the framework of a Minsky burlesque show for what is basically a serious play, and the production must embody this association or the full meaning of the play will not be realized.

Other entertainment forms that have been used as clues to the commanding image include:

> ***Commedia dell' arte*—commonly used in interpreting much of Molière and some of Shakespeare**
>
> **Motion pictures—which furnished techniques used in planning the Broadway production of *Angel Street* [see Gallery of Production Interpretations]**
>
> **Court masques—on which have been based productions of *The Tempest, Twelfth Night, A Midsummer Night's Dream,*and other plays**

Nightclub or cabaret comedy could be used to visualize for modern actors the intimacy of the actor-audience relationship in the Restoration theatre. Interpretations of plays might also stem from analogies with puppet shows, Christmas pantomimes, minstrel shows, operettas, revues, circuses, carnivals, and masquerades.

Other Forms of Designed Action

Rituals, ceremonials, dances, and similar forms of composed action may relate revealingly to a playscript and the realization of its rhythmic form. Thus Tyrone Guthrie's mass-like *Oedipus Rex* at Stratford, Ontario, ". . . makes no attempt whatsoever to persuade the audience that what is seen and heard is 'really' happening. Throughout, actors commemorate and comment upon the sacrifice of Oedipus . . . in a manner analogous to Christian priests' commemoration and comment upon Christ's sacrifice."[8] And the producers of T. S. Eliot's *The Cocktail Party* saw sections of it as ritual and performed some of the social chitchat in the cadences of liturgy, as can be heard in the original-cast recording of the play.

CONFLICT AND COMPETITION

Conflict and competition are central to most plays, and thus a good source for associational analysis lies in other conflict forms such as war and competitive sports and games. For instance, strategy is closely associated with conflict and in drama often involves feats of skill; thus, imagining that dialogue and movement are like "juggling, walking on eggs (or hot coals), treading water," may help to pin down the motivational basis for a scene and suggest its inherent rhythm.

Floor plans of Mordecai Gorelik's settings for *Golden Boy* said, "life is a fight," through their boxing-ring image (see page 139 for Gorelik's description); variations on this image suggest meaningful patterns of action for all aspects of a production of this play, including sound and lighting effects.

Clifford Odets' *Golden Boy,* a play which literally involves prize fighting in its subject matter, is metaphorically a statement of the conflict between spiritual and material values. In Act I, scene 4, the metaphor is presented in microcosm as a "battle" between two of the central characters—the scene repeats the pattern of the larger structure. Lorna, mistress of Moody, the fight manager, has been sent to seduce the hero Joe into abandoning his music for the fight game; Joe, meanwhile, is struggling within himself to come to a decision. Stage directions for the scene read:

A few nights later. Joe and Lorna sit on a bench in the park. It is night. There is carousel music in the distance. Cars ride by in front of the boy and girl in the late spring night. Out of sight a traffic light changes from red to green and back again throughout the scene and casts its colors on the faces of the boy and girl.

There are no specific cues indicated by the playwright for when the light changes, when the cars ride by or how fast they should seem to be going, or how loud the music of the carousel should be; these important artistic choices are left to the director.

The director who sees sound effects and lighting simply as added literal content for the sake of realism might:

Play the carousel record at a predetermined volume under the entire scene

Use a continuous background of traffic noise—cars passing —under the entire scene

Have the traffic light change color regularly at a typical realistic interval throughout the scene

and thereby impose a regular, dulling rhythm on the scene.

On the other hand, the director who sees the sound and lighting effects in this scene as part of the image of the conflict that is the play would:

Carefully select nostalgic carousel melodies and vary the volume so that the music "enters" to set a mood for the scene and especially to participate in Joe's speech explaining how music means more to him than money and boxing.

Cue the cars to "enter" when they can be used to motivate a reaction or set a new mood, and notice the fact that by

> **the end of the scene the cars, which Joe calls "poison in my blood," should have drowned out the carousel music.**
>
> **And finally, he would time the traffic light so that the changes would subtly punctuate the moments at which the relationships between the boy and girl change, thus accenting the structural units of the scene.**

He would thereby bring to life the rhythm organic to the scene. Thus the author's image would be expressed not only in the lines, but in the lighting and sound effects, as the following sections of the sound-and-light script illustrate:

Part of a sound-and-lighting plot for *Golden Boy*.

9

LORNA: Success and fame! Or just a lousy living. You're lucky you won't have to worry about those things....
JOE: Won't I?
LORNA: Unless Tom Moody's a liar.
JOE: You like him, don't you?
LORNA: [*After a pause*] I like him.
JOE: I like how you dress. The girls look nice in the summer time. Did you ever stand at the Fifth Avenue Library and watch those girls go by?
LORNA: No, I never did. [*Switching the subject*] That's the carousel, that music. Did you ever ride on one of those?
JOE: That's for kids.
LORNA: Weren't you ever a kid, for God's sake?
JOE: Not a happy kid.
LORNA: Why?
JOE: Well, I always felt different. Even my name was special—Bonaparte—and my eyes...
LORNA: I wouldn't have taken that too serious....
[*There is a silent pause. Joe looks straight ahead*]
JOE: Gee, all those cars...
LORNA: Lots of horses trot around here. The rich know how to live. You'll be rich....
JOE: My brother Frank is an organizer for the C.I.O.
LORNA: What's that?
JOE: If you worked in a factory you'd know. Did you ever work?
LORNA: [*With a smile*] No, when I came out of the cocoon I was a butterfly and butterflies don't work.
JOE: All those cars... whizz, whizz. [*Now turning less casual*] Where's Mr. Moody tonight?
LORNA: He goes up to see his kid on Tuesday

LORNA: Tokio says you're going far in the fighting game.
JOE: Music means more to me. May I tell you something?
LORNA: Of course.
JOE: If you laugh I'll never speak to you again.
LORNA: I'm not the laughing type.
JOE: With music I'm never alone when I'm alone—Playing music... that's like saying, "I am man. I belong here. How do you do, World—good evening!" When I play music nothing is closed to me. I'm not afraid of people and what they say. There's no war in music. It's not like the streets. Does this sound funny?
LORNA: No.
JOE: But when you leave your room... down in the street... it's war. Music can't help me there. Understand?
LORNA: Yes.
JOE: People have hurt my feelings for years. I never forget. You can't get even with people by playing the fiddle. If music shot bullets I'd like it better—artists and people like that are freaks today. The world moves fast

The process by which associational analysis discovers how all the literal elements of a play integrate into a pattern of figurative meaning is illustrated by the following discussion of *Born Yesterday,* in which such analysis integrates the dramatic action, designs the setting, chooses props, and in effect organizes the whole in terms of images analogous to the play's conflict. Thus far, the plays used for examples have been largely serious "classics"; however, the Broadway farce—the kind often thought of as "merely commercial"—proves that the usefulness of the ideas being presented here is by no means limited to dramatic masterpieces. Another example demonstrating the same point will will be found in the discussion of *Angel Street* in Part Four.

The literal contents of the setting are described in the script as follows:

> ***Born Yesterday*** **happens in the sitting room of Suite 67 D, a large part of the best hotel in Washington, D. C. A duplex apartment, a masterpiece of offensive good taste, colorful and lush and rich. A circular staircase and balcony. On balcony a huge ottoman and two doors leading to bedroom suites. A swinging door leads to the service wing. Two main doors open onstage. Two French doors leading to terrace. A large window with drapes and curtains. In the distance the Capitol dome can be seen. An ornate fireplace with complete equipment, a Swedish modern sideboard, a bookcase unit (empty), a sofa and coffee table, an end table with drawer, ornate single pedestal round top table and three ornate chairs. On the table is a gilded telephone.**

Any ground plan of this set must be an arrangement of these physical facts. Here is an arrangement incorporating all the facts in a useable plan offering a variety of playing areas:

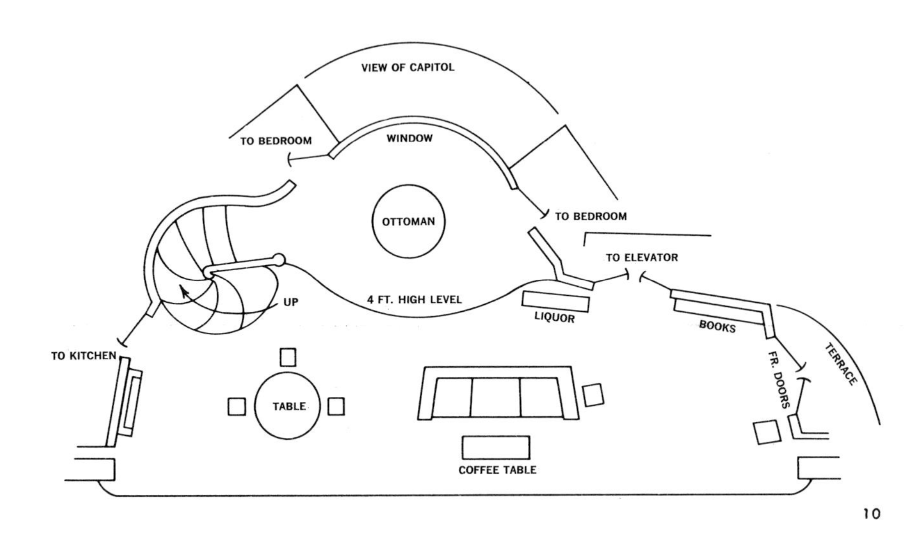

10

If, however, we regard the physical facts as the embodiment of an idea, then the idea—the commanding image—will arrange them in a meaningful pattern. We begin to grasp the commanding image of *Born Yesterday* when we notice that in the play an expensively vulgar hotel suite, used for immoral purposes involving lobbyists and legislators, is turned into a battlefield by a reforming civics teacher and his pupil.

The idea of a battlefield suggests dividing the physical facts into two rival camps.

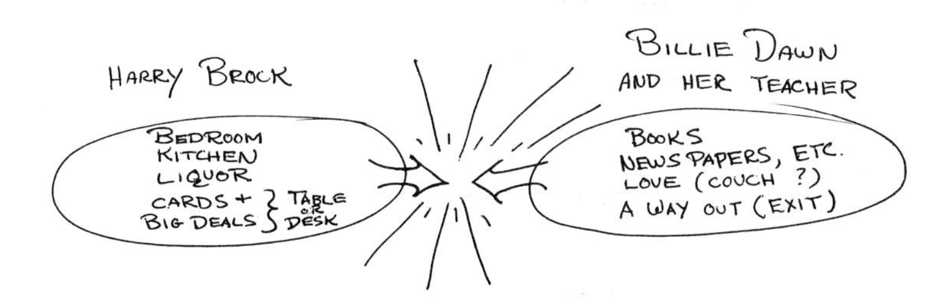

The ground plan of the Broadway production looks as if it might have been developed from just such a scheme:

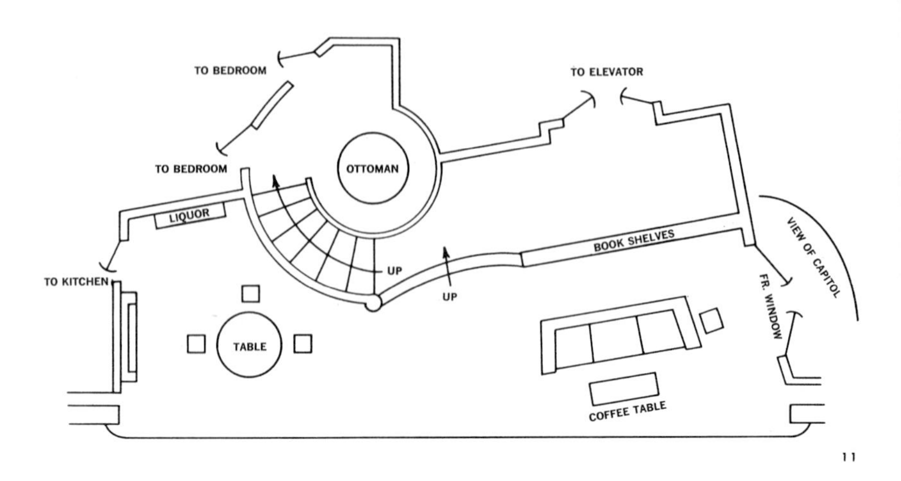

11

This ground plan divides neatly into two camps with a no-man's-land between. Down left, the couch and coffee table will become the classroom where Billie Dawn learns to value herself, her rights, and her country. Down right is the camp of Harry Brock's predatory materialism. Here drinks are drunk, cards played, food eaten, contracts signed; upstairs on this side the bedrooms complete the equipment of the war profiteer's temporary office-harem. The curtain rises on Donald Oenslager's setting for the Broadway production:

12

The effect of the decor, its tone set by the delightfully vulgar MGM-baroque stairway, is instantly comic. Soon after Harry Brock enters we realize that this is less an expensive hotel suite than it is a crooked junkman's idea of heaven. Brock brings his harem with him—his kept woman, his kept lawyer, later his soon-to-be-kept congressman.

When Brock hires a young not-to-be-bought liberal journalist to educate Billie, the battle lines are quickly drawn.

Act II shows the couch area in use as a schoolroom, with Billie discovered surrounded by piles of books and magazines, newspapers spread around her as she busily circles with red pencil the parts of her reading she wants explained. The impact of the schoolroom image might be made more striking and funnier by the addition of some bulkier props: a small rolling blackboard, for instance, and some hanging charts of government and corporate ("It's a cartel!") structures. These could surround Billie and cut her off from Brock. She might try to hide behind them when he approaches to strike her at the end of the act.

The final victory of Billie and her teacher could leave Brock sitting defeated in the schoolroom. If some of the books were stacked on the upper level above the couch, Billie could topple them onto the sulking junkman—a final exit gesture of victorious contempt.

The commanding image in this production of *Born Yesterday* might be stated thus:

> **An adult education course in civics precipitates a revolution in the harem.**

ANALOGIES TO OTHER ARTS

Other art forms: painting, architecture, music—can help the interpreter to define the play.

Painting

Painting often gives theatre artists ideas for pictorial composition and for period details of props, costumes, etc. It can also give actors a "feel" for the period, as Kim Stanley testifies (quoted by Lillian Ross writing in the *New Yorker*):

> Before we opened in *Cheri* in New York, I went to the Phillips Gallery, in Washington, and as I was standing there looking at the Renoir painting "Boating," I actually got feelings from it that I could use in my part—the way those women lean on their hands, the physicalization of it, that lovely roundness they have. Paintings can be a help if you're working on a part that doesn't belong to your own immediate background. Each age has its own texture. . . . I consider my portrayal of Lea in *Cheri* a failure, but I couldn't have gone on to play Elizabeth in *A Far Country* if it hadn't been for my experience in that part. . . . There had been nothing in my life to give me references to an aristocratic or upper-middle-class European style and milieu. . . . [I spent] days and days in the New York Public Library working on the part of Elizabeth. I not only read Freud's writings about Elizabeth, I also looked at late nineteenth-century Viennese prints that showed the physical constriction of the women of the time, and studied the social context for the part. . . . I was quite pleased when several Viennese members of the audience at *A Far Country* came backstage to congratulate me on

what they said was my convincing portrayal of an upper-middle-class Viennese woman of that period.[13]

One can also discover in painting aesthetic points of view which may make the interpretation of a play more concrete.

What the playwright assumes for a visual impact of his play is often difficult to see completely in reading the script. Painting—a single unchanging graphic image which need not, as a play must, be studied as a form developing in time—can instantly evoke responses that sum up the play's impact. Thus:

Yves Tanguy called this work *"Encore et toujours"*—"Still and Forever"—but it might also be called *Waiting for Godot.*

14

The critical attitude toward society implicit in Congreve's wit—and easy to miss when one is accustomed to thinking of the Restoration as an amoral period—is made visible by examination of the "diverting" pictures produced by Hogarth in the same spirit:

15

A painting *technique* may also provide an interpretative approach to a theatrical production. Thus the principle of collage became the production mode of the opera *The Ballad of Baby Doe,* for collagelike thoughts were evoked at the very birth of the opera. When the subject of Baby Doe Tabor was first mentioned to the librettist, John Latouche, "some memory stirred," and fragmented images assembled themselves in his mind:

Tabor, the fabulous silver king of Leadville, the man who had helped build Denver . . . The Tabor Grand . . . The

> **Brown Palace Hotel, with its lobby inlaid with silver dollars . . . The Tabor Grand Opera House, still doing service as a movie house . . . Baby Doe, a curvaceous, blue-eyed image once seen printed on a beer tray, a titled profile in mildewed Sunday supplements . . . Bryan . . . Free Silver. . . .**[16]

Donald Oenslager's design concept corresponds in spirit and even in many details to these first impressions of Latouche: the scene designer calls his sets "collages of nineteenth-century Western American Art":

[17]

The small pictures in the proscenium arch are photos of Tabor's holdings, changed as the scenes change. The sets themselves combine photographic with engraved and other illustrative effects of the period.

18

Besides analogies to already existing works of art, the interpreter may make use of visualizations he creates himself—scrawls and "doodles" in which he attempts to capture the characteristic qualities of the play. By resisting the urge to draw pictures of the set immediately, he may instead try to sharpen his sense of the play by setting down graphic impressions of how the play "feels"—in color, shapes, lines, textures (the technique of collage might be useful here, for one might create an associational abstraction out of bits and pieces of various materials that together seem to be "like" the play). In such freely created "doodles" may be found colors, shapes, textures, perhaps movement patterns that could later be used in the production; perhaps none of these things will emerge, yet the very act of creating such a visualization may add to the grasp of the commanding image.

Architecture

> **. . . alone of the Arts can give space its full value. . . . Painting can depict space; poetry, like Shelley's can recall its image; music can give us its analogy; but architecture deals with space directly; it uses space as a material and sets us in its midst. . . . Space affects us and can control our spirit . . . excites a certain mood in those who enter it.**
>
> ***Geoffrey Scott***[19]

Experienced in time and space as one moves through it, the "frozen music" of architecture is still another form of designed action analogous to drama. Architecture can contribute to both aesthetic and literal analysis, for as Siegfried Giedion puts it:

> **However much a period may try to disguise itself, its real nature will still show through in its architecture, whether this uses original forms of expression or attempts to copy bygone epochs. We recognize the character of an age as easily as we identify a friend's handwriting beneath attempted disguises. It is as an unmistakable index to what was really going on in a period that architecture is indispensable. . . .**[20]

For instance, a feeling for how Racine's *Phaedra* resembles baroque architecture in its approach to and treatment of its material can help a modern interpreter grasp those aspects of the author's image that are intimately involved in the aesthetic point of view Racine shared with his audience, the *Zeitgeist* of the age of Louis XIV.

One of the passionate interests of Louis XIV was *forcer la nature,* and the formal gardens of Versailles, designed by Le Notre, assert the Sun-King's power to force nature herself to conform to the will of the absolute monarch. In the same way, baroque architects created effects which seem to defy nature in both the character of the medium and the law of gravity—granite columns which writhe, marble which swirls into flamelike forms, and bulging walls of masonry that seem to be in constant motion.

To the theatre audiences of Louis XIV's Paris, nature threatening to burst the bonds of human control would have the potential of a thrilling, terrifying spectacle, and this is just the spectacle which Racine exploited by concentrating on the anguished struggles of his characters to hold their all-too-human natures in check. In *Phaedra* he dramatized the awful power of sexual passion, a theme sure to interest a court in which boudoir intrigue and affairs of state were often intermingled.

Since the essential events of the play are changes in the psychological states of the characters, Racine was able to provide lightning-fast shifts in direction for his twisting plots as the characters explore every possible way to escape the inevitable. Chaos threatens at any moment to burst all restraints: Phaedra's reply to the insistent questions of her confidante early in the play is characteristic:

> **You press my silence like a rotten fruit.**
> **If it should burst, what do you think you would see?**[21]

The same sudden changes of direction and pressure against restraints can be seen in the swelling curves and the graceful but tense gyrations of baroque architecture—illustrating, as Earnest Mundt puts it in *Art, Form, and Civilization,* "how far inner forces can be allowed to develop without entailing anarchy."[22]

23

The Ascension of Mary.

24

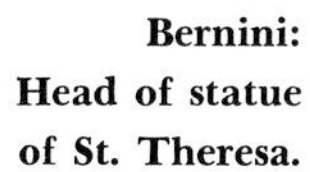

Bernini: Head of statue of St. Theresa.

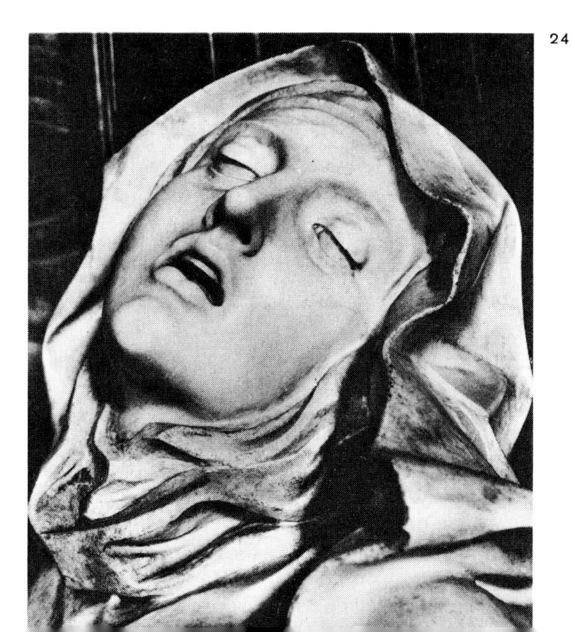

Stage directions in Jean-Louis Barrault's published *mise en scène* of *Phaedra* (Paris, 1946) reveal how a sensitive interpreter reacted to the script by demanding of the actors the same violence and writhing energy that baroque architects built into walls and columns, the same ecstatic agitation carved into baroque sculpture:

> **Phaedra twists around and now has her back three-quarters turned to the audience. She seeks out Hippolytus' eyes. . . . With an abrupt and savage twist of his neck, Hippolytus turns his head. . . . She rears back. Then she straightens up and, about three feet away from him, her body wrenched like a twisted stalk. . . .** [25]

But all this violence, to be acceptable to the baroque audience, had to be held under control; as Barrault says of another part of the same scene: "While exuding sensuality, the characters must lose nothing of their grandeur and nobility." Just as the architects contained all the seething energy of their forms within the strict laws of their classicist aesthetic—preserving order, balance, and symmetry even while pushing to the outer limits of the rules—so Racine used the very severe limitations placed on playwriting for the creation of telling effects.

The limitations were practical as well as aesthetic. For instance, a modern playwright dealing with Phaedra might show the love-sick, distraught queen in wild disarray as a result of her passion, but Racine could not consider such a treatment. Not only did aesthetic decorum forbid it, but Racine's courtesan actresses would never appear without every hair in place, bejewelled, and beribboned in glorious formal dress and makeup. Far from merely enduring this fact of theatrical life, Racine called attention to it to illustrate Phaedra's disturbed state of mind in her second speech in the play:

> **These jewels weigh upon me and these veils press me down.**
> **Whose hand has tied this hair about my head?**
> **Whose thoughtless hand bent on weaving knots?**
> **There is some conspiracy to work me harm.**

Thus Racine makes dramatic capital of the fancy dress that his actresses and audiences expected by showing Phaedra writhing in anguish, imprisoned in her finery. Recognizing Racine's method, a modern interpreter might well discard any idea of free-flowing Greek costumes in favor of a stiff, jewel-encrusted, and whaleboned dress from which the actress could struggle to free herself.

The interpreter might better understand the annoying (to him) regularity and rigidity of *Phaedra's* verse if he saw it, like the classicism of the architecture, as part of Racine's baroque commanding image. Racine gloried in his ability to use the alexandrine, strictest verse form of a form-conscious age, and to make its most finicking rules serve his purposes. One of the requirements was that each line end a logical sequence of thought with no carry-over into the next line. A carry-over (*enjambement*) was a defect of style that Racine's audience would instantly recognize. Only in very special cases did the rules permit a carry-over, called a *rejet*. Racine used his audience's awareness of these rules to make an emotional point, providing a famous example of the successful use of the *rejet* in the second act of *Phaedra*. Here, in her passionate scene with Hippolytus, Racine has Phaedra make five *rejets,* thus indicating to his audience that she is so carried away by emotion that she cannot control her speech as a great lady should—an example of baroque chaos-within-limits.

Periclean Greece: Nature is a serene balance of forces . . . "Nothing in excess."

Baroque France: Nature is tension forced into balance

. . . *"Forcer la nature."*

Thus, an appreciation of the ways in which *Phaedra* is like baroque architecture provides a clearer understanding of Racine's classicism and how its performance style differed from the ceremonial restraint and dignity demanded by the works of Aeschylus and Sophocles.

> **A scene . . . in Racine . . . closes for a time a series of negotiations between wild beasts.**
>
> ***Jean Giraudoux*[28]**

> **Oh, this is no gentle warmth that tingles in the veins. This is Venus clawing at the belly of her prey.**
>
> ***Phaedra, Act I, scene 3***

A quick comparison of baroque architecture with that of Periclean Greece makes the difference quite clear.

Architecture relates to drama in a much more obvious way. The environment in which a dramatic action takes place often presents us with the need for creating effects like those produced by architectural environments. The dramatic interpreter, perhaps even more than the architect, must be sensitive to the emotional impact of architectural forms.

Thus, for *Death of a Salesman* Arthur Miller asks for "towering angular shapes . . . surrounding it on all sides. . . . A solid vault of apartment houses around the small fragile-seeming home." Early in the play, Willy says: "There's not a breath of fresh air in the neighborhood. . . . They should've had a law against apartment houses. . . . Smell the stink from that apartment house! And another one on the other side." Although he asks that these apartment houses disappear for certain scenes, Miller's overall intent calls for the background to create an image of oppressive mass and enclosure—clearly a problem to be solved by analogy to experience with architectural effects.

Jo Mielziner, whose settings tend to depend on painter's effects and atmospheric lighting, created a smoky background having an effect of flatness:

29

Mario Vanarelli, by stressing sharpness of detail, chiaroscuro, and texture, designed apartment houses looking more like the author's "solid vault."

30

For a similar problem in ominous and oppressive mass, the architect–scene designer Joseph Urban relied on his experience with masses of masonry and their emotional effects in designing Strauss' *Electra* for the Metropolitan Opera:

31

The architectural effect of a setting may quite effectively mirror the interpreters' entire concept of a production, down to the attributes of its acting style, as can be seen by comparing the settings for the two New York productions of Eugene O'Neill's *Desire under the Elms,* which offer a particularly illuminating demonstration of how profoundly the scenic architecture may affect the total meaning of the production.

O'Neill's great ambition was to write tragedy using American materials; in his writing he frequently used the Greek classics as models. The classic image is clearly visible in the formality and simplicity of O'Neill's own sketches of the setting for *Desire under the Elms*:

32

O'Neill's setting is essentially symmetrical, with the front gate downstage center dividing the stage into two almost perfectly balanced halves, the whole framed by symmetrical, brooding elm trees.

Robert Edmond Jones, who both designed and directed the 1926 premiere production, based his design on O'Neill's sketches, but carried the classical symmetry even further by eliminating the porch O'Neill had sketched:

33

Completely symmetrical except for a freer use of the foliage of the mothering elms, Jones's stark and simple farmhouse epitomizes both the puritanical New England environment of the play and the author's intention to write a tragedy on classical lines.

Essential to the O'Neill-Jones conception is the four-sectioned front wall of the house, by means of which the rooms of the interior were closed from view when not in use.

The elimination of this solid facade is the most important change made by Mordecai Gorelik in designing the 1952 revival of the play at the ANTA Playhouse:

34

The reason for this change is clearly implied in Gorelik's note on the design:

> **The design responds well to a complex light plot required by the time-sequence of the script and a constant shifting of attention from room to room and from interior to exterior.**[35]

As is his custom, Gorelik worked very closely with the director, so all the changes can be assumed to be a part of a new production concept, one which saw the play as best suited to being treated "like a legend—a story from the remote past." Because the script makes constant reference to the weather, the new concept also placed heavy emphasis on an expanse of sky in which atmospheric effects could register strongly. In addition, the design allowed for the sort of cinematic continuity of action through a multi-roomed setting that has at this writing become almost conventional on Broadway. Apparently to add still another acting area, the porch that Jones had eliminated was brought back in the new design, creating unusual sight-line problems, the solution of which played an important part in determining the final form of the set. The elms were stripped of almost all their foliage and formed a rather harsh frame for the house.

Without doubt, Gorelik's open-roomed house is a smoother operating, more efficient "machine for theatre" than Jones's set with walls that had to be moved with each change of scene from one room to another. But what of the emotional impact of these two concepts and their relation to what O'Neill had in mind?

The "feel" of the O'Neill-Jones designs, the impact of their stark, simple shapes under the overhanging softness of the foliage, is tragic in the Greek manner, with a hint of the Freudian content of the play.

The "feel" of Gorelik's 1952 design, with its far more

complex silhouette suggesting a more rambling farmhouse than the simple frame building of Jones's design, with its gaunt elms framing the exposed guts of the house, is rather melodramatic in the more recent style of *A Streetcar Named Desire.*

The two scene designs—in their appearance, approach to scene changing, and in other implications for their respective productions—have two distinctly different rhythms; each set of interpreters chose the one they felt corresponded to the rhythm of the playscript.

Each design implies a different style of acting:

> ***Jones's set:*** **Asks for a realism which is simple and clean-lined in the way it makes its points—a sort of classical realism.**
>
> ***Gorelik's set:*** **Has (as he admits) "a superficial air of naturalism" despite the basic theatricalism of the conception, implies realism in the Method manner—characterized by elaboration of detail and a quality of improvisation—a realism different from the one O'Neill wrote for in 1924.**
>
> ***Question:*** **Can the interpreter "modernize" the acting style in this play without altering the essential effect of the production, or is this, like a Tennessee Williams style production of *Oedipus Rex,* a question of two different ideas of Man?**

Where the Gorelik design suggests the shape of the house by means of a roof line and a chimney, the O'Neill-Jones concept shows the upstairs rooms actually roofed over behind the facade:

36

This design factor helped produce the effect that Joseph Wood Krutch found to be most expressive of what O'Neill had achieved in writing the play:

> **He has learned . . . that spirits cabined and confined by very virtue of the fact that they have no outlet explode finally with the greatest spiritual violence. . . . The idea of setting the stage with a single permanent scene showing one end of a farmhouse, and of removing sections of the wall when it becomes necessary to expose one or more of the rooms inside . . . is admirably calculated to draw attention to the controlling circumstances of the play. It is a story of human relationships become intolerably close and limited, of the possessive instinct grown inhumanly powerful because the opportunities for its gratifications are so small, and of physical passion terribly destructive in the end because so long restrained by the sense of sin. . . .[37]**

It can be questioned whether the effect of "spirits cabined and confined" can be achieved with scenic architecture in which the rooms are open to the sky, as in the design of the 1952 revival. Does not Jones's use of walls and ceilings add to the feeling of puritanical repression and concealment so important to the play's meaning? May they not also add to the audience's sense of seeing something terribly private when the walls of the rooms are removed? Can the same effect really be achieved by lighting alone, no matter how complex the light plot?

One factor important in evaluating the differences between these two productions has been left out of this discussion: the factor of relative scale. Jones designed his production for a small stage in a small theatre. This identical design, moved on to the stage of the ANTA Playhouse, might well look insignificant; scaled up to fit the large Broadway stage, the resulting farmhouse might look too spacious. Further, it may well be that the impression of "spirits cabined and confined" was significantly increased by the audience's own confinement in the intimate Greenwich Village theatre; this effect might be most difficult to secure in any more spacious auditorium. Thus, at times in spite of the interpreters, the effect of architecture can become part of a production's meaning.

The interpreter of plays, then, needs many and varied experiences with the emotional dynamics of architecture, for these may in many ways apply to the meaning of dramatic productions.

Music

Music, because it develops in time like drama, can offer analogies for use in getting close to some of the least tangible yet vital aspects of dramatic meaning.

> **We have found that a good script, a play that is well written for acting on the stage, contains time spans—movements and rhythms—comparable to those in music. . . .**
>
> ***Jacques Copeau***[38]

> **The performance of the play is clearly analogous to the performance of a symphonic piece of music. By the time the play is ready, if it is properly rehearsed, the diverse voices, the group of people who are playing the thing, will have found a music for their parts. . . .**
>
> ***Tyrone Guthrie***[39]

> **Opera taught me to shape my plays into recitatives, arias, duets, trios, ensemble finales and bravura pieces to display the technical accomplishments of the executants. . . .**
>
> ***G. B. Shaw***[40]

The interpreter needs a wide listening experience in music; especially he should have a feeling for the emotional effects and how they are created through the composer's use of rhythms, keys, modes, voice qualities of individual instruments and their combinations, harmonic effects and so on.

With this background the interpreter may be able to define the dramatic principles of a script in musical terms.

For example, the question of how to treat the chorus in producing Greek tragedy is partly answered by noticing that the characters in Aeschylus are featured instruments in a concerto, while the chorus is the orchestra—the musical matrix within which the action is revealed. A director steeped in realism finds the chorus an antique curiosity, not part of the "real" drama; he tries to correct this by treating the chorus as individuals reacting in realistic detail to the action: he treats the choral lines as conversation. Keeping the concerto idea in mind shows why the chorus is dramatically necessary, how it must behave as a group (orchestra), and why its voices and movement must be lyrically designed.

In like manner, seeing Maeterlinck's *The Intruder* as a tone poem suggests concrete techniques for its production. The instruments in a composition like Debussy's *Nuages* concentrate on an emotional aura—the mood in which they are caught holds their attention so that they examine it and hold it in suspension, rather passively, lest it change—they do not (as do instruments in more traditional works) erect a musical structure of melodic line or polyphony; they establish and sustain a quality of emotion. Seen as a tone poem, *The Intruder* is not a "static" drama which ought to have its scanty plot emphasized, its lack of activity compensated by imposed movement, and its seemingly vague characters made more convincing by sharply defined interplay and motivation; rather, its action is preoccupied concentration on the atmosphere of mysterious and impending doom. Thus, ordinary plot development merely gets in the way, and the characters become unconvincing if they are *not* vague with one another because they are "listening" to something else.

Again, the sense of structure is extended when *King Lear* is viewed as a fuguelike development of main themes. The basic principle of the fugue, statement in one voice and imitation in another, is apparent in the Lear and Gloucester interweaving of plots. The leading theme— concerning a royal father and his daughters—is "stated" in the Lear story line and is picked up and imitated with variation in the Gloucester story of a subject father and his sons.

At a deeper and more pervasive level, the main theme may be viewed as one of misconceived values or aberrations of reality. This is introduced when Lear sees his traitorous daughters as devoted children, while Cordelia appears to him as a faithless monster, and the loyal Kent as a villain. The theme is immediately restated in slight variation with Gloucester's error of taking Edmund to be his loving son and Edgar the murderous one. With the reintroduction of the supposedly faithless Kent disguised as a trusted servant, a motif of loyalty mistaken for villainy and treachery posing as devotion is established from several "voices." Against this theme develops a variation of it in degrees of real or feigned madness wrongly construed. The fool's gibbering reveals intuitive wisdom, Mad Tom is really sane, the mortal storm in Lear scatters his logic but stirs him to deeper insights into truth, and so on. To this structure is added still another counterbalanced scheme—the eyes of Lear's mind are at last opening as he discovers reality, while Gloucester is literally blinded as he grasps the truth. Thus a contrapuntal composition is developed through pitting one variation of hidden truth against another and weaving them together in an ever richer momentum of images. Blindness, real and spiritual; masquerades, literal and figurative; madness, actual and pretended are woven into a "polyphonic" structure, and these contra-themes are finally resolved in the closing "chord" of the play in which all the voices have either dropped out or come into consonance with Lear.

This musical view of *King Lear* gives its interpreter a perspective of its unifying principle and protects him against the tendency, so natural to drama, of losing sight of the whole as he labors over such things as the meaning of individual lines, costume details, and setting problems.

At a more specific level, thinking of the actors as voices in a musical composition suggests that analogies drawn from musical experience can aid in the casting of the play:

> **Shaw, writing *Pygmalion,* created—among other things—a "bravura piece" to "display the technical accomplishments" of an actress who, in playing Eliza Doolittle, must be capable not only of imitating both Cockney dialect and perfect English diction, but of progressing from nasal, buglelike tones to the variety, mellowness, and wider range of a viola.**

> **The rallying calls to arms that Shakespeare put in the mouth of Henry V demand an actor whose voice can be an inspiring trumpet sounding sennets and flourishes.**

VERBALIZING THE IMAGE

Thus far the presentation of associational analysis has illustrated how, by finding analogous experiences in life and in the other arts, the interpreter is able to clarify and perhaps discuss his sense of the play—his feelings about what the experience of the play is like. It has been shown that images can be found which lead the interpreter to artistic decisions of all kinds, from casting and movement patterns to the selection and design of a specific property or setting, from the effect of a single instant in the performance to that of the entire production. These images do not have to be verbalized in order to aid the interpreter in his exploration of the nonliteral meaning of a script. However, at some point in this process, to crystalize his own realization of meaning and especially to aid in the communication of this to others, it is obviously valuable for the interpreter to be able to say vividly in words what the play is like.

Many interpreters find it a worthwhile discipline to try to capture the import of the play by verbalizing it in some simple statement or statements. As the artistic import of the play is a metaphorical image, it may best be summed up in metaphor statements. This suggestion is not the same as the more common one that the interpreter "sum up the meaning of the play in a simple one-sentence assertion." Such advice may be dangerous, for it too commonly assumes that the essential meaning of a play can be explained—converted, that is, into a simple expositional message. Of course there are plays whose essential communication can be summed up in a declarative sentence, but these works do not disprove the truism that artistic meaning eludes reduction to simple statements of fact.

Various workers in the field have also placed rather strict limitations on the length of verbalizations, in the manner of the contest formula of "twenty-five words or less." But, though the discipline of brevity quite often leads to greater precision of statement—important in making concrete decisions about a complex work—such demands can and do lead to pointless oversimplifications and to fruitless and frustrating labor. The verbalization of the commanding image is first and foremost an analytical technique, a method of work, not an end in itself. As in the case of all the techniques herein described, the essential standard for judging the value of such verbalizations is "Does it *work?*" not "Is it a clever, beautiful, or poetic statement?"

It is also very important to notice that to try to state an image for a play is to assume that the play in question has one that can be identified in this manner. The discovery and statement of a central metaphor which alone creates a form for the production is an exciting but rather rare possibility—as rare as the few playwrights who have executed works with such a flawless and firm sense of artistic purpose that the commanding image of their creation can be verbalized. Moreover, in the case of a labyrinthine play like *Hamlet,* while one feels its essential unity, to capture its central meaning in a verbal metaphor might well be impossible.

Ultimately, the only complete way to express the commanding image of a play is through a complete production of it. While recognizing this fact—which is basic to the theory of theatrical meaning contained in this book—one must also observe that the *attempt* to verbalize the image of even so complex a play as *Hamlet* can be most illuminating and useful to the interpreter.

Both the difficulties and limitations of verbalizing dramatic meaning must be borne in mind when reading the following three examples of such verbalizations. They have been chosen to illustrate various aspects of the problem. For example, *The Boor* shows that an image statement can be brief and precise, but that it must above all express the spirit of the play, while the metaphor statement discussed for *Oedipus Rex* shows that a key image can be very useful without necessarily being immediately clear in its implications to anyone but the interpreter who has verbalized it. Finally, the analysis of *The Cherry Orchard* provides a commanding image which cannot be confined to the "twenty-five words or less" approach.

Chekhov's delightful little farce *The Boor* might be reduced to a "message" like "love conquers all" or "never underestimate the power of a woman," but such statements get the interpreter nowhere. "Love conquers all" fails to distinguish *The Boor* from hundreds of other comic and serious plays that arrive at the same cliché *(Romeo and Juliet,* for example), nor does it point the way to a production concept for the play.

The kernel of *The Boor* is its hilarious viewpoint, its attitude, and this can be stated by means of short, farcical metaphors:

Smirnov, the boorish bill collector, is a bull in a china shop.

Elena, the dimpled little widow, is a Venus flytrap with delusions of being a shrinking violet.

And the play as a whole is
a love match between a sentimental King Kong and "Our Gal Salome."

These images do point the way to a production concept, suggesting ideas for casting, characterizations, movement patterns, setting, costumes, and makeup. Smirnov is seen as a massive, hulking, hairy, bellowing actor in a fur coat—beneath whose rough exterior beats a heart of pure mush; Elena is seen as instinctively seductive and strong-willed despite her affectations of celibate mourning and retiring delicacy; the setting is seen as made up of fragile bits of Victorian bric-a-brac in which Smirnov has a sense of being trapped even before he is actually caught.

It should be noticed that the mixture of animal, plant, and human images does not matter in the least if the combination is expressive and accurately interprets the script. Artistic perception is bound to the law of emotional association—not to logical connection. We have all been taught that a mixed metaphor is a sin; this notion is right as it concerns consistency, but wrong in that it confuses literal meaning and art. The commanding metaphor—the dominant image—must be single in its effect, but as in dreams the parts integrate on an emotional basis. Logic is secondary.

Earlier, the "privacy" of some images and the difficulty of communicating them to others was mentioned; the verbalization of the commanding image serves primarily to crystalize the image for the interpreter, and the statement that results may not be entirely clear to others without further elaboration. Even the simplest of such statements organizes for its creator a whole complex of production ideas—specific ways of executing the production which may be apparent only to the person who creates the verbalization and to those who can see all its implications.

For example, the commanding image of Sophocles' *Oedipus Rex* might be stated: "This play is a searching movement toward a blinding light." This statement, to the interpreter who made it at least, includes a complete production concept and also implies the play's literal "message" that "illumination—in this case, self-knowledge—may be almost unbearable." The discussion which follows describes the production concept implicit in the metaphor statement. It also deals with some ideas seemingly implied in the metaphor which the interpreter should reject, as well as problems involved in the execution of the production concept so that it expresses the play and not some imposed pattern of ideas.

Developing the Idea

Probably most of the intended effect of *Oedipus Rex* could be created by any performance which emphasized powerful characterization and clearly articulated the plot. Since so much is expressed in what Sophocles has given the characters to *say,* even an oratorio reading might project a good share of the play's meaning. However, expressive actor's movement and choreography were part of the playwright's intent; in fact, there are moments in the play where the real dramatic impact of the scene is not contained in the dialogue, but in the implied mimetic action. There is no question that physical staging created to complement and clarify the psychological action of this tragedy would help it to produce its maximum impact on an audience. The image of "a searching movement toward a blinding light" can lead to such staging, to a pattern motivated by the demands of character and situation which at the same time expresses the form of the action implicit in the script.

The searching movement is of course a psychological form, not a physical one. If one sought to express such a form in a film, an obvious technique to employ would be the familiar one of moving the camera in closer and closer to the searcher's face as he neared the truth, so that the audience would feel an ever increasing involvement and intimacy, resulting in a building of tension and excitement. A similar stage effect can be achieved by moving an actor toward the audience. By letting Oedipus come closer and closer to the audience as the plot approaches its crisis, the audience would tend to feel a mounting tension like that in the camera-work example, and the living presence of the suffering Oedipus would add to the impact of the device. Thus, the main psychological action of the play could be strengthened by this physical action. Properly worked out, then, this use of space and distance could be a key principle in the staging.

The effect requires a movement which is fundamentally perpendicular to the proscenium arch, suggesting that the play is better suited to an open or platform stage than to the typical proscenium theatre—not a surprising thing, considering the 64-foot open dancing circle for which it was written. A stage platform and an enveloping auditorium like that of the Stratford, Ontario, Shakespeare Festival Theatre would be best suited to the production concept of *Oedipus* being worked out here. On such a stage Oedipus could be brought forward into the midst of the audience, a decided advantage in creating the buildup of audience involvement desired.

Two demands of the script provide a condition which, in a theatre like the one in Canada, automatically sets up movement patterns which tend to flow up and down stage. First, there is the palace door, which would have to be at the rear, and would form an upstage pole for movement; second, there is the only other specific acting area demanded by the script—the altar at which Jocasta prays. This altar, as will be shown, is more important than one might at first think, and since it can be put to excellent use somewhere at the foot of the platform, in that location it could form a downstage pole for movement.

The altar, so frequently used in Greek plays, was probably at the center of the orchestra in fifth-century B.C. Athens. In *Oedipus Rex* Sophocles takes advantage of its presence by representing it as belonging to the god whose ministers first announced the curse; the altar is dedicated to Apollo, the god of reason and light, the patron of the Oracle of Delphi, and hence the crucial deity for this play—a point which was probably obvious to Sophocles' audience, but is apt to be missed by a modern one. The playwright makes a particularly strong dramatic effect with the altar in scene 3. Jocasta comes to the altar, places offerings on it, and prays fervently to Apollo that she and her husband be delivered from defilement. As if in answer to her prayer, the Corinthian Messenger arrives while she is still at the altar and announces the death of Oedipus' "father." But with characteristic Sophoclean irony, what appears to be good news is in reality tragic, and it is clear that before the Messenger has finished, Jocasta knows the truth. Her prayer to escape from the ancient curse predicted by the sun-god has been answered by the selfsame god—with doom. Clearly, the altar is an important property, and will work best in a prominent position.

Sophocles uses the altar, with all its rich implications for the tragedy, as the means of introducing Jocasta's enlightenment. It thus suggests itself as an emotionally charged object, which the audience associates with Apollo and the fateful enlightenment directed principally at Oedipus. Since this is the case, it seems sensible enough to make even further use of Sophocles' device, and have Oedipus, too, learn the final truth somewhere near the altar. This idea happens to provide a plausible reason for moving Oedipus closer and closer to the audience as he nears his discovery, and makes a complete staging plan possible.

Staging the Play

At the rear of the jutting stage, great doors lead into the palace of Thebes. When Jocasta rushes off the stage for the last time, these doors are left open, and the audience can see that they open into dark corridors. The play's action moves from this darkness to an area emotionally connected with the "light" of tragic revelation—in this production, to the altar at the downstage tip of the platform, far from the palace doors. A scenic structure created out of ideas derived from the image "a searching movement toward a blinding light" can now be illustrated:

41

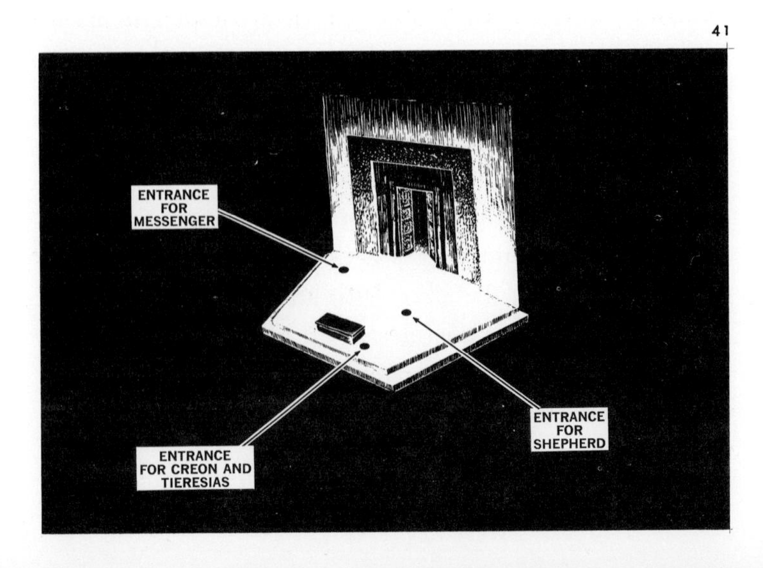

Each of the aisles is to be used as if it leads to a particular offstage place—a convention adapted from the supposed practice in the theatre Sophocles wrote for, wherein entrances from one side were traditionally associated with travelers from foreign lands, and opposite entrances with people coming from the city. In this proposed production, the point at which each character mounts the stage is significant in employing the image, for the way Oedipus can most convincingly be moved closer and closer to the fatal altar (and the audience) is for each successive character to enter at a point further downstage; simply by truthfully relating to these people, Oedipus ends up where the final emotional effect requires him to be. No arbitrary "blocking" is necessary.

Of course, no audience today will automatically sense that the altar has special significance; an association between the altar area and the imminent fate of Oedipus needs to be implanted in the minds of the audience early in the play. Some of the early scenes can help establish a subconscious association long before Oedipus plays his climactic moments there.

Creon initiates these associations on his first entrance. Bringing the advice of Apollo's Oracle at Delphi, he makes his entrance from the aisle that ends at the altar. He stands there during his first speech, but moves upstage to Oedipus' side at the palace doors during his second speech:

> **Is it your pleasure to hear me with all these**
> **Gathered around us? I am prepared to speak,**
> **But should we not go in?**

Oedipus puts aside Creon's caution, and the Oracle's words are made public by Creon, now standing beside Oedipus at the palace doors. The search begins.

A second and very important association of the altar with the sought-after truth comes with the entrance of Tieresias. The prophet enters, or rather seems to rise up, in front of the altar as he is led up concealed steps just in front of the stage. The blind old man remains near the altar throughout his scene. Oedipus' respect and concern at the beginning of their encounter motivate him to come down to meet the seer, and the agon is played far downstage, close to the fatal altar—for Tieresias, in his anger, brings Oedipus face to face with the truth. But Oedipus angrily refuses to recognize the truth and stalks upstage to the palace, leaving Tieresias to disappear down the steps, an ominous threat on his lips.

Thus far, associations with the altar have been based on the implications of these two early scenes, but as we have already seen, Sophocles' use of the altar for Jocasta's prayer scene makes the connection with the god of enlightenment quite explicit. This is one of those places where crucial mimetic action is clearly implied by the playwright. As Sophocles sets it up, the Corinthian Messenger arrives while Jocasta stands at the altar, and as she listens silently to the Messenger's story, she apparently remains there. Though the playwright gives her no words to declare it, it is clear that Jocasta knows the truth before the Messenger has answered all of Oedipus' questions, for when Sophocles finally has her speak, it is to try to dissuade Oedipus from searching any further for what she has already seen. In other words, Jocasta's movement of realization must be performed in silence. Now, the implied staging seems to call for Jocasta prominently visible, but concealing her discovery of the truth from Oedipus. In this proposed production the Messenger would enter at a point about halfway downstage, causing Jocasta to turn her back on the altar and the largest portion of the audience. At the moment when the truth hits her, she recoils and turns suddenly away from Oedipus to conceal her emotions from him, and thus faces the audience again. This turn reveals her emotions and focuses the audience's attention on her and the pitiful remains of her prayer offerings. Some such movement is needed to dramatically articulate this important "unwritten" plot development. After a moment of dialogue behind her that adds no really new information, she is called upon to play her final scene.

By this time, the significance of the altar is felt by the audience; the setting is ready for the fall of Oedipus. Jocasta's lamenting exit has left him with the Messenger more than halfway downstage of the palace; the Old Shepherd comes on stage from the "Theban" aisle at a point downstage of them. Closing in to question him, Oedipus is led still closer to the altar. As he begins to realize where his questions are taking him, the tormented king turns away from the others on stage. Perhaps he stares out over the altar into the darkness of the theatre, as if asking his question of the god. At each answer, he moves as if drawn or pushed closer, and standing just where Jocasta and Tieresias had stood, he comes abruptly to the end of his journey—to an illumination so painful that it sends him screaming back into the echoing darkness of of the house of Laius. When Oedipus returns after having destroyed his own sight, the figure of "a searching movement toward a blinding light" is complete.

Dangers and Advantages

While the script is not so simple that merely staging it as a series of scenes moving steadily downstage will add anything to its impact, the fact remains that Oedipus' main action is strictly that of a search, that the central imagery is all connected with light, dark, sight, and blindness, and that "a search toward a blinding light," simple as it is, expresses a major portion of the form-giving aspect of the play. Thus, if an evocative use of stage space can enhance this image, so much the better.

However, as has already been noted, the movement of this search is emotional, not literal; obviousness and illustration must of course be avoided. The problem is to create a performance which *feels,* to the audience, like a movement along a path leading into terrible danger; the performance should not look like such a movement. The greatest danger of staging the play "as if on a path" lies in the possibility of turning the physical action into a diagram, into an illustration, thus moving away from dramatic action toward exposition. Therefore, Oedipus must not perform "searching movements," stalking about the stage like Hawkshaw the Detective or Fearless Fosdick hunting clues. Nor should the director let his desire for dramatic effects trap him into accenting the great moment of "blinding light" by suddenly hitting Oedipus' upturned face from all sides with white-hot light. Though it seems to grow out of the image, such an effect only calls attention to itself and merely illustrates, instead of enacting, the image. The "blinding light" in this play does not suddenly appear; it has always been there for Oedipus to find.

This production concept for Oedipus may seem to some reminiscent of the autocratic director's *regiebuch* which demands that the actors, puppetlike, carry out every minute gesture of its blueprinted performance. Such a rigid use of even the most ideal performance concept is always possible, since there are directors who freeze their ideas too early in the production process. This commanding image and its rather general "performance" ideas developed gradually, as they might in rehearsal, out of many examinations of what the playwright had done. Actual production with living rather than imagined actors would necessarily produce changes. It is assumed that the director, accustomed to this, keeps his eyes and mind open—and probably keeps his mouth shut about the details of the schemes in his head. He uses his preconceived ideas as a general guide for himself rather than as a set of blueprints to be followed with blind, uncreative obedience.

But an image and a plan like this one, kept largely in the director's mind as he works, can be most useful in helping the actors in their creation. It can, for example, provide the director with concrete terms for describing the effect he wants—terms the actor can grasp and perform. How, for instance, is Oedipus to react at the moment when he discovers the terrifying truth—when he stands in the blinding glare of it, to use the image? The image of the truth as a blinding light suddenly reached leads to analogies a director can use to evoke ready responses from any actor, and which can be made deeply effective by a talented one:

> **You almost know now—you are staring, eyes wide with horror as the last bits of cloudy uncertainty are blown away. When you get the last fact, it is as if, after a long groping journey down a dark tunnel, after your eyes have grown used to the dark, you turn a corner and suddenly find yourself staring straight into the blinding, exploding brightness of the noonday sun. For the first shocked instant you stare helplessly, then the searing pain gets to you. Perhaps you scream, trying with your fists or arms to shut out the light as you stagger from the pain. . . .**

Once more let it be said that these images are based on the playwright's own, for Sophocles has Oedipus blame Apollo for his suffering—Apollo, god of divine vision and light, of the sun. This key image must be a main concern of any modern production concept, for the ncessary associations with the gods are no longer automatic. In Sophocles' audience, this device must have struck powerful and familiar chords of response, for it belonged to a tradition centuries old in the Greek way of thinking. In *The Iliad,* for example, Ajax raises a cry that might be Oedipus expressing his own compulsion to know: "Make the sky clear, and grant us to see with our eyes. In the light be it, though thou slay me!"

Finally, it should come as no surprise that a detailed production concept can be developed from this play and shown at every point to have grown out of Sophocles' own lines and images. Since the birth of dramatic criticism *Oedipus* has been regarded as probably the most perfectly written play in all dramatic literature—which is to say, in other words, that it is the most precisely proportioned and perfectly designed image in the history of the theatre.

A Final Example of Verbalizing the Image

Recalling Gordon Craig's injunction against reading stage directions, it is interesting to discover that the whole form and idea of Chekhov's complex play, *The Cherry Orchard,* can be found and finally verbalized by recognizing that the stage directions at the beginning of each act are images rather than mere lists of appropriate technical details:

> ***ACT I:*** **A room which has always been called the nursery. . . . Dawn, sun rises during the scene. May, the cherry trees in flower, but it is cold in the garden, with the frost of early morning. Windows closed. Enter Dunyasha with a candle. . . .**

Things are mentioned which are not apt to be represented on the stage: frost, for example. We are being told how Chekhov sees the play—not what the audience is to find in the set. This is a stage direction conceived by "the inner eye." Thus, the cherry orchard and the house are one idea —the estate, the cradle, the "nursery" of this milieu. The season of the year and the time of day are one idea:

> ***Dawn*** ***Awakening and Homecoming***
> ***The Estate Remembered and Rediscovered***

> ***ACT II:*** **The open country. An old shrine, long abandoned and fallen out of the perpendicular; near it a well, large stones that have apparently once been tombstones, and an old garden seat. The road to Gaev's house is seen. On one side rise dark poplars, and there the cherry orchard begins. In the distance a row of telegraph poles and far, far away on the horizon there is faintly outlined a great town, only visible in very fine weather. It is near sunset. . . . All sit plunged in thought.**

In the foreground, time past, decay; in the distance, the time to come, the growth of a new order. The future has already made an inroad—telegraph poles—on the past. The shrine, the tombstones, the orchard are all one figure;

they are slipping away, "fallen out of the perpendicular," eroded, sinking into shadow in the sunset of the old order. Between daylight and dark—a pause, a time for remembering:

> ***Dusk*** ***Remembering and Waiting***
> ***The Estate Fading Away***

> ***ACT III:*** **A drawing-room divided by an arch from a larger drawing-room. A chandelier burning. The Jewish orchestra, the same that was mentioned in Act II, is heard playing in the ante-room. It is evening. In the larger drawing-room they are dancing the grand chain. The voice of Pistchik:** ***"Promenade à une paire!"*** **Then enter the drawing-room in couples. . . . Varya is quietly weeping and wiping away her tears as she dances. . . .**

The gloom is held back by elegant ritual, French phrases, champagne, but the gaiety is hollow:

> ***Night*** ***Celebrating and Sorrowing***
> ***The Estate in a Final Futile Burst of Life***

> ***ACT IV:*** **Same as in First Act. There are neither curtains on the windows nor pictures on the walls: only a little furniture remains piled up in a corner as if for sale. There is a sense of desolation: near the outer door and in the background of the scene are packed trunks, traveling bags, and so forth.**

> [The dialogue indicates that it is Fall, October, bright clear sunshine. And at the end of the play:]

The stage is empty. There is the sound of doors being locked up, then of the carriage driving away. There is a silence. In the stillness there is the dull stroke of an axe in a tree, clanging with mournful lonely sound.

[The aged servant, Firs, appears, mutters pitifully about being left alone, and lies down, motionless.]

A sound is heard that seems to come from the sky, like a breaking harp-string, dying away mournfully. All is still again and there is nothing but the strokes of the axe far away in the orchard. Curtain.

The "nursery" is being abandoned, summer is gone, and the orchard is being destroyed—all components of a death that is now clear—in a bright, cold light. Gently, finally, the last cord breaks; the old order is gone:

A New Day ***Leave Taking and Sleep***
The Estate Abandoned

A close study of the stage directions of *The Cherry Orchard* reveals much about the rhythmic form of the play and the meaning created by that rhythm. The pattern of the play is circular, beginning with awakening from sleep and ending with the return to sleep.

The essential "statement" of the play, distilled act by act from the directions and their relation to the action, might be stated as follows:

ACT I: **On the threshold of our final joy, we welcome one another with hope—for all that we have loved is still at hand.**

ACT II: **But our joy is wistful and sad, for darkness is falling on our estate.**

ACT III: **Into the night we laugh; our final hollow effort to deny**

ACT IV: **. . . that a new day has come, a cold, clear day that stares pitilessly down on the now abandoned life which once we knew.**

As has been suggested, to reduce a play to a short statement in order to lay bare its meaning is to risk laying it bare with the useless effect of flaying it, of stripping it of its real flesh and substance. A bald statement of literal message gets the interpreter nowhere, but a verbalization of meaning which identifies the compositional core of an apparently plotless play like *The Cherry Orchard* is an achievement that is certainly practical. The "statement" of the play offered above gives the interpreter not only the basic mood and purpose of each scene, but provides him with a way of judging every element; from Madame Ranevsky's first reaction on returning to the "nursery" of her youth to the why and wherefore of using the gay-sad music of an uprooted people for the "celebration"—every detail, no matter how literal and how minute, can be evaluated in terms of its contribution to Chekhov's commanding image.

A Note of Warning

It has been pointed out that a single-minded—Commanding Image or Bust—search for one central metaphor often leads to abortive, frustrating results; it may also lead to jumping at "inspired" but unfortunate conclusions. It is far wiser, in using the discipline of associational analysis, to follow the common practice of concentrating on climactic scenes first. If these can be vividly interpreted, the scenes that lie between can be filled in with comparative ease. And metaphors for these particular scenes are likely to occur even if an image for the whole is not found; if enough of these are discovered, they may fall suddenly into a larger and more significant pattern.

A conscientious interpreter might prepare for rehearsals by finding as many different analogies as he can for each essential part of the play, as Burgess Meredith did before directing *Ulysses in Nighttown*:

> Meredith, planning the rehearsals, made a breakdown of the script into fifty-six separate scenes and to each scene he gave a color, a volume for voice, a psychological adjustment for each actor in the scene, the intention, the physical characterization (usually by reference to a well-known painting of Michelangelo, Hieronymus Bosch, Rembrandt) the geographical equivalent, the type of theatre style. For instance, the geographical equivalent of the opening scene between Buck Mulligan and Dedalus is "A conversation between Teddy Roosevelt and Lord Byron." The one for the opening of Act II, Lynch and Dedalus discovered in the brothel, was "Two Harvard men in Harlem on Saturday night."
>
> The purpose of the "breakdown" was to work out a set of references, in and out of the theatre, so that the actors could make an emotional bridge to the subtleties of Joyce.[42]

Other directors, less self-consciously systematic, prepare themselves in a more general way, allowing images for particular moments to emerge out of their responses to the rehearsing actors and what they feel the scene needs. Whether one works from impromptu reaction or carefully preplanned images matters not at all. What does matter is that finally the playwright's intent is brought vividly to life.

RESPONSIBILITY FOR THE MEANING OF THE PRODUCTION

Although the questions of what the play is about and its theatrical context have been given only outline treatment here, a thorough understanding of the playwright's intention involves these questions as much as the matter of figurative meaning and form. What this section has primarily tried to do is show how associational analysis works and how it grows naturally out of the very principle on which dramatic meaning operates.

The listing of so many sources of useful analogies for interpreting plays seems to imply that the interpreter ought to be a Renaissance Man, a person of appallingly comprehensive culture. Can one really expect the theatre artist to be so marvelously sensitive and experienced in music, painting, architecture, and so on? Well, though it might be an unattainable ideal, it would be useful. In any case, the more avenues one has explored, the more experience one can tap, the more raw material he has with which to create. The stultifying results of cultural overspecialization for any theatre artist are thus too obvious to need further spelling out.

But cultural narrowness is not the only problem. There is a growing tendency toward overspecialization within the theatre itself. This results in assertions of individual artistic sovereignty by the specialists, and in attitudes toward their work which conflict with the essential effort to have the production make sense through unity.

For once the meaning of the production has been decided—the image found—strict limits have almost automatically been defined within which all the artists involved must work. The definition of these limits can hardly be left to a committee of autonomous individualists. Therefore, artistic pride, professional practice, and union regulations aside, there is little doubt that ideally, the conception and execution of the production should be dominated by one artist.

Many a designer, having created a wonderful "machine for acting" based on his own conception of the staging of a play, has been left frustrated and enraged on discovering that the director has used his set as little more than a backdrop, playing scenes in front of scenery designed to contain and support them. Many directors, on the other hand, have had to battle against designers' notions which, though in themselves beautiful, would destroy the play—often by their very beauty. Though there have been cases of equal collaboration, this demands an extreme of matched brains, talent, and points of view, which is hard to find even in marriage.

The separation of production design into two specialties—directing and scene design—is an operational convenience; in view of the enormously complicated and difficult tasks involved in modern play production, no one can quibble with the obvious need for such a convenience. However, this separation has been elevated into an aesthetic principle: "Two heads are better than one" is the gist of the argument, and what may happen with "too many cooks" is ignored as an undemocratic sentiment.

There can be little doubt that better theatre results when one mind dominates. It is surely no mere coincidence that the greatest eras of dramatic art were dominated by men who were in complete command of their medium, as witness Aeschylus, Sophocles, Shakespeare, and Molière—actor-director-playwrights all.

When the theatre began to be dominated by interpreters rather than playwrights, the most influential ideas about production theory came from men who were capable of conceiving the entire production: Goethe, Wagner, Saxe-Meiningen, Appia, Craig, Stanislavsky, and later on Louis Jouvet, Robert Edmond Jones, Lee Simonson, Mordecai Gorelik, and others all directed, designed, and theorized in terms of the entire production. Although (as will be shown later) the theories of some of them were unfortunately picture-oriented—an unavoidable result of the proscenium theatre in which they worked—the continued validity of many of their ideas can be attributed to their wide range of interests and abilities.

The great significance of this seems lost, however, and the training of theatre artists increasingly stresses the wrong sort of specialization—a specialization that increases the difficulties between directors and designers by reducing the amount of their shared experience, and hence the number of areas in which the mutual exchange of ideas is possible. Training of this sort also creates artists who cannot help but be self-indulgent, who know no other goal than that of a brilliant performance in their specialty—who cannot be expected to know when their brilliance destroys rather than illuminates the play.

Any mutual exchange of ideas implies, in addition to

the common goal of communicating the play, a common language; actors and directors, designers and technicians, though their special skills and our producing system require them to specialize, *should have identical training in interpretation.* At every level of training, ways must be found to keep each specialist aware that what he is doing is essentially the same as the work of other specialists, that is, to place emphasis on the essential oneness of the task.

In both the professional and university theatres there is an ever-increasing number of designers who do not know what it feels like to act in the scenery and costumes they design, of directors who have had no personal experience in the meaningful use of color, light, line, and mass, and of actors who are ignorant of how to make effective use of costumes and scenery and who alter movement and business with no understanding of the plan of the whole.

The training and working attitude of theatre artists should reflect the truth that all of them are doing essentially the same thing, so we can say that:

> **A good designer designs a set which channels the movement of actors, determines the visual image projected to the audience, and so, in large part, directs the play.**
>
> **A good director, working with the actors on their interpretation, controls the movement of the action and so develops the audio-visual image projected to the audience, and, in large part, designs the production.**
>
> **And finally, a good actor, responding to the import of what the director and designer have conceived, brings to life the work of all his collaborators, and in doing so, enacts the playwright's commanding image.**

It is meritorious to insist on forms. Religion and all else naturally clothes itself in forms. All substances clothe themselves in forms; but there are suitable true forms, and then there are untrue unsuitable. As the briefest definition one might say, Forms which GROW *around a substance, if we rightly understand that, will correspond to the real nature and purport of it, will be true good; forms which are consciously* PUT *round a substance, bad. I invite you to reflect on this. It distinguishes true from false in Ceremonial Form, earnest solemnity from empty pageant, in all human beings.*

THOMAS CARLYLE[1]

PART THREE: The Evaluation of the Production

This book has presented an approach to the analysis and definition of the dramatic experience—of the work as a whole. By treating artistic meaning as definable rather than mysterious, the metaphoric principle also offers criteria more specific and defensible than some of those commonly used for the evaluation of dramatic productions.

Recently the emphasis in critical theory has been on the relativity of artistic meaning; "levels of meaning" and "varieties of artistic experience" are key terms in this trend. Unfortunately this emphasis has seemed to some to justify the shutting off of serious criticism of whimsical, hasty, and poorly reasoned interpretations with the claim that any "meaning" a work can be made to express is as significant as any other.

The metaphoric approach to meaning recognizes and accounts for the variety of meanings a play may communicate, but sees a nucleus of meaning which is essentially the same for most people and to which all other meanings relate. In other words, there is a core of original meaning around which cluster a limited number of possible valid productions, all having quite a bit in common with one another because of their nearness to the orginal intention. Further out are an infinite number of possible productions which are rather more interested in using the script as a point of departure than in interpreting it. The metaphoric approach also makes clear that the literal meanings of a script are not the only ones that can be discussed, and that metaphoric import can be both described and, through associational techniques, precisely realized. Realized—*not* explained, for just as a joke explained is no longer a joke, a metaphor explained is no longer metaphorical in effect.

Thus, the metaphoric approach also recognizes as valid such a statement as, "I interpreted it that way because that's the way I feel it." However, this concept of meaning gives the interpreter a way, through association, of communicating the specific facets of the way he feels the play as a whole. By citing images analogous to the whole or particular scenes, the interpreter can point to the sources of his feeling, and so can evaluate and discuss its validity. Assuming that he also analyzes the literal content, the interpreter can therefore profitably discuss every aspect of his interpretation. For the artist who is trying to teach the performance of his art, there is enormous value in such discussion. Not only can he explain his reasoning, he can reveal *how* he is able to distinguish a good artistic effect from a bad one.

By logically justifying the analysis of dramatic meaning and showing that the interpretation of a play can be profitably discussed, the metaphoric approach also implies that the incompetent performer can no longer safely dodge questions aimed at evaluating his work with the pat evasions: "a work of art means different things to different people"; "it is impossible to say what a work of art means"; "everyone has a right to his own interpretation."

THE QUESTIONS TO BE ASKED

Metaphoric analysis, as has been shown, can provide useful answers to such questions as: What was the author's intent? How was his intent communicated to his audience? —and in regard to new productions—How does this new production communicate the author's intent to his new audience? To these may be added the classic questions which may be asked of any work of art: What is the artist trying to do? How well did he do it? Was it worth doing?

These form the basis for all the more particular questions which must be asked in both the creation of the dramatic production and the criticism of its performance. The combinations and working of these questions may vary, as in the following discussion, but the basic considerations remain the same.

WHAT DOES THE PLAY MEAN?

In applying the metaphoric approach to criticism, the critic, like the theatre artist, looks for the commanding image of the play, both in reading the script and watching the performance. To those who object that one need not bother to read the scripts of most plays that are produced in our commercial theatre, let it be admitted that the approaches described in this book will not be uniformly useful to everyone. It is also necessary to make a distinction between the informative and valuable work of the reviewer, whose assignment is chiefly to report theatrical events and his immediate reactions to them, and the function of the critic—who may be the same man—who selects plays for careful examination and takes the time to give them more considered evaluation. Furthermore, it must be acknowledged that it is possible for some critics to see the performance of a play they have never read, and yet be able to distinguish so carefully between script and production that in effect they "read" the play as they see it. One may admit, in other words, the existence of critical genius. Bernard Shaw, for one, seems to have had this talent, but other examples do not come readily to mind without some reservations.

The conscientious critic, then, should read the play and form his own idea of the play's essential meaning before he evaluates the theatrical performance; unless he does so, he has no real standard against which to measure the interpretation. The critic may read the play before seeing it, using his own image in evaluating the performance while he sees it, or he may read the play after seeing it, checking to see if his own reactions to the script coincide with what he saw enacted; but whatever his preference, he should, if at all possible, actually read the script before writing his criticism.

In reading the script, the critic should be able to employ the same techniques of literal and associational analysis as the performing interpreters, which strongly indicates that the artistic training of the critic should be the same as that of the interpreters themselves—already the custom in some countries where such training is more systematically professional than in our own. One would also expect to find among the better critics men who also had experience as artists in the medium they judged. Goethe, Lessing, Zola, Shaw, Stark Young, Harold Clurman, James Agee, and others could be cited to confirm this expectation.

Having decided on his interpretation of the play's meaning the critic is in a position to judge what the theatre artists presenting the play were trying to do.

DOES THE PRODUCTION HAVE AN IMAGE?

In cases of productions which shun "affectations" like interpretation in favor of "letting the play play itself," the critic will often find a pointless performance which he can write off as such. However, the possibility must be recognized that talented, hardworking performers responding intuitively to a good play may communicate its meaning—create its image—in spite of their belief that they have not bothered to analyze it. Therefore, the critic must treat the *performance* as the essential evidence of interpretation and not be misled by what its producers think or say they have done.

IS THE IMAGE THE ONE IN THE SCRIPT?

Pointless, "imageless" productions may appear in various disguises. Stylizing setting and costumes in the manner of Greek vase painting, medieval tapestries, the *commedia dell' arte,* or Kabuki may create the impression that the production has a design; in actuality these are often forms of decoration imposed on productions with no organic image.

The critic must distinguish productions whose style embodies the play's commanding image from those whose form came out of discussions such as:

> ***Business Manager:*** **Our last two Shakespearean plays have been "Globe" staged—it's time for a change.**
>
> ***Designer:*** **The modern dress bit is old hat—Say! How about *Twelfth Night* in the style of an antebellum coming-out party? Southern belles, Kentucky Colonels—the plantation in the moonlight.**
>
> ***Director:*** **Banjos ringin'—Feste singin'—and Aguecheek doing a drunken cakewalk with Toby Belch! Why not?**

One excellent way to distinguish a good from a bad image is to notice if every aspect and detail of the production fits together without seeming forced or farfetched—or without calling undue attention to itself.

For example, the idea of doing *The Way of the World* in modern dress—as if it takes place in the jittery and brittle society of the TV–Movie–Ad Agency set—has many attractions:

Congreve's polished, witty lines might sound right as the artificial chatter of the cocktail lounges.

The basic drives of the characters—for money, power, and love—ring true for the denizens of the analyst's couches.

The loose morality of Congreve's society fits neatly into the gossip columnist's image of the way of the Broadway and Hollywood world.

But, on the other hand, the entire plot of Congreve's play hinges on an idea of the status of women utterly different from that of the career woman, starlet, or sex kitten. Mr. Fainall attempts to extort a fortune from his mother-in-law by threatening to ruin his wife's reputation; he threatens a divorce suit based on the then scandalous disclosure that she had had an affair before their marriage. This threat could hardly be taken seriously by the super-sophisticates of the proposed "show-biz" translation. Other aspects of the position of women in *The Way of the World* would produce similar incongruities. Thus, though the surface decoration of the play might be translated to the new setting, key motivations of the story line and the play's acid portrait of a society are made to seem absurd. Therefore, to do the play this way would be a bad choice of image.

The organic theory of play production and the concept of stylization, which came with it, are the two proudest accomplishments of the modern theatre. These ideas have seemed to set the modern era apart from the past, giving it a claim to progress and inventiveness. But, in spite of their greater sophistication and awareness in matters of interpretation and in spite of their endorsement of the organic theory, many modern producers have adopted, ironically, an essentially external, nonorganic approach—for "stylization" indicates an act of *doing* something *to* the play:

> **Oftentimes the designer . . . decides deliberately to change the realistic forms to nonrealistic ones which will interpret the play in a more individualistic style. . . . Stylization means simply that the style of presenting the object is emphasized more than the object so that one becomes conscious of the designer's style as a mode of expression in itself. . . . Although stylism takes its impetus from the script . . . its scope depends largely upon the designer's own personal choice of emphasis which he somewhat arbitrarily superimposes on the script in order to facilitate the audience's interpretation of it.**
>
> ***From a current book on scene design***

The designer "somewhat arbitrarily superimposes" his ideas instead of finding what grows naturally out of the script. Looked at in terms of the organic theory of play production, the very words used here to define stylization are a condemnation of this approach.

If arbitrary and arty selection of stylizations will not give point to a production, neither will the "realism" of taking a movie company to Verona or to Scotland create a more meaningful production of *Romeo and Juliet* or

Macbeth. Here, too, the manner of presentation tends to be emphasized more than the play itself—literalism, too, is a form of stylization.

To begin the production process with a concern for style is an act of confusion, for the form of the production should be the solution to the problem of communicating the image of a particular play to a particular audience. To decide on a style first is to have found a "solution" before the problem has been defined—to prescribe a cure before the diagnosis.

The playwright has something specific to communicate; his play is formed as a solution to the problem of getting his dramatic idea across. Thus, in the larger sense, style is the result of purpose and is organically part of the play's meaning. Since purposes are infinitely various, styles are also infinitely various. To classify scripts and productions in terms of "isms" oversimplifies the problem of analysis and forces production into stereotyped forms.

A production may succeed in persuading most of an audience that its wrong image is right. According to Eric Bentley, who had to see it twice before he could pin down what was wrong, the Elia Kazan production of *Cat on a Hot Tin Roof* is a case in point:

> **The relation of play and production . . . seems to be a relation of exact antithesis. When the curtain first goes up, Mr. Williams sends on stage a girl whose dress has been spilled on at dinner; but, so far as the audience can see, the dress is as spotless as it is golden and sparkling. It is the same with her personality and character. From the author: a rather ordinary girl, *bornée*, perhaps stupid, shabby-genteel. From the production: Barbara Bel Geddes, the very type of non-shabby, upper-class gentility, wholesome as a soap ad. It is the same with the other characters. . . .**

> **It is the same with the whole evening: the script is what is called dirty, but the production—starting with the Mielziner set and its chiefly golden lighting—is aggressively clean. . . . Giving a "clean" production to a "dirty" script he [Kazan] has persuaded people that the dirt is unimportant. The show *looks* wholesome; therefore, it is.**[2]

No matter how persuasively executed, then, a wrong image remains wrong and a legitimate target for the conscientious critic.

CAN THE INTERPRETER USE THE PLAY TO CREATE A NEW IMAGE?

Reinterpretations of classics—from Orson Welles's "Fascist" *Julius Caesar* through Kurosawa's samurai film version of *Macbeth,* titled *Throne of Blood*—have raised the thorny critical question: Does the interpreter have the right to use the playwright's work as a springboard for a new idea of his own?

Obviously, the original intention of many plays may not necessarily be as worthwhile for future audiences as for the audiences the playwright had in mind. Some period plays are revived only for their value as entertaining curiosities; no one is seriously disturbed by a radical departure from the playwright's intent where the play is a second- or third-rate work. But when, as often happens, an interpreter creates a startling new image for some great play, important questions of art are raised.

In the 1957 Baylor University production of *Hamlet,* which was quite honestly advertised as a new version, separate facets of the central characters were played by two or more actors, after the manner of experiments in the 1920s by Evreinov *(The Theatre of the Soul),* Susan Glaspell *(Overtones),* and others. In the case of this *Hamlet* and other conceptions involving drastic rewriting and/or re-arranging of the author's idea, the critic is forced to ask, "Was it worth doing?"

For when an interpreter undertakes to redesign or re-write a play like *Hamlet* he invites comparison with the original, just as Shakespeare's play was no doubt compared to earlier versions. Thus, some potentially embarrassing questions become perfectly legitimate for the critic to ask: Was this production a more valuable experience for the audience than an equally well-performed rendition of the original would have been? Is the "new" play a *better* play than the original? Is it even as good?

Polish producer Bohdan Korzeniewski, speaking of Kurosawa's film, *Throne of Blood,* as an example of creative liberty, aptly summed up the cost of such freedom:

> **When we have granted the producer the liberty of creation, we demand of him a creative responsibility. . . . Hence, we do not consider it a violation of Shakespeare to transfer, for instance, the action of *Macbeth* from Scotland to Japan. All we ask is that the producer, having thus adapted Shakespeare's play to Japanese customs, should not hide the fact—as Kurosawa has not hidden it—that he has used Shakespeare to create his own work, and we expect him to prove, by his production, that he had the right to do so.**[3]

Proving this right is a heavy obligation, for it is possible that a new and startling image, however brilliantly executed, may still result in a production that must be considered inferior art.

HOW WELL IS THE IMAGE EXECUTED?

Once the intended production image has been determined and evaluated, the critic is ready to judge the quality of its execution. For the purposes of the present discussion, we must take for granted talent and hard work—though these are perhaps the major factors in any interpretation—and the emphasis must be placed on the ideas which the talent and hard work are made to serve.

Production ideas can fail as interpretations through being unnecessarily illustrative, distorting the proportions of the playwright's image, being precious, or in other ways failing to communicate the script to the audience. By asking himself questions about these things, the critic can estimate how well the interpreters' job has been done.

DOES THE PRODUCTION SUFFER FROM ILLUSTRATION?

Bad acting, bad playwriting, and bad designing commonly stem from the same fundamental errors, and the tendency to "illustrate" is one of the most prevalent. In falling into the error of illustration or demonstration, the actor shows us what an angry man looks like instead of convincing us that he is angry; the playwright writes conversation in which people explain characters and situation instead of creating action that reveals situation and character; directors and designers use signs and symbols which merely tell us what the play is supposed to mean instead of creating forms which powerfully enact it.

Leopold Jessner's famous use of steps in his 1921 *Richard III* production is a case in point. In Shakespeare's play, Richard metaphorically "ascends" to the throne by a bloody path and then in a series of defeats is quickly "brought down" again. Jessner turned this image into literal description by placing on the stage a bloodred pyramid of steps; these Richard actually mounted in successive phases until he won the summit, the throne. Jessner's setting was criticized for creating clumsy conditions which caused the leading actor to trip and fall, but this mechanical flaw might have been avoided simply by using wider treads on the steps. The basic conception itself was a more serious blunder: Jessner sought to underline the intent of the author by creating a scenic diagram of the rise and fall of Richard—a literal "graph" of Richard's fortunes, which the audience was to consciously recognize. Thus the setting was an eye-filling allegory of political success and failure. But the play is in no way allegorical; Jessner added an extraneous element which, though ingenious and fascinating, stole the audience's attention from Shakespeare's intended center of interest, Richard the man.

Similar staging ideas, legitimately motivated and unobtrusively carried out, can be used meaningfully to support the author's intent: Laurence Olivier uses levels most effectively throughout his film version of *Henry V*. In the St. Crispin's Day speech, for example, Olivier has Henry rise from intimate conversation with a few friends to a public address rallying the whole army; the climactic build of the lines is staged with changes in level that most of the audience would never consciously see as anything but realistic action. Henry begins on the ground, addressing a small group of nobles; as he warms to his subject, walking through the camp, more and more soldiers gather and Henry's voice rises in volume; to be visible to more of them, the King walks up on to a wagon and uses it as a speaker's platform—his delivery quite naturally expands from a conversational to an appropriately flamboyant oratorical style. The audience, seeing nothing unusual or distracting in these actions, is unaware of the devices being used, yet feels their effect.

As was the case in Robert Lewis's use of the "flowering tree" image in *My Heart's in the Highlands,* Olivier's visual metaphor of a dramatic climax was built out of carefully selected realistic details, plausibly motivated. The failure of Jessner's design might be attributed to its doctrinaire abstractness.

Other examples of the difference between metaphor and illustration can be cited. For the 1937 Group Theatre production of *Golden Boy,* Mordecai Gorelik conceived a metaphor which embodied the play's central conflict, and which grew naturally out of the playwright's own images. The struggle between material and spiritual values is handled in the script with a series of hard-hitting, fast-moving, and well-defined scenes, which build steadily in tension. For the young boxer, Joe Bonaparte, life is a fight in every respect, and the producers of the play saw that its essential impact could be heightened by staging all of it as if the combatants were in the ring:

> **The production of *Golden Boy* was shaped in part by the fact that I chose the image of a prize ring for the whole play. It was as if each scene were set up in a prize ring, as if a gong rang for the start and finish of each scene, as if the actors came toward each other from opposite corners each time. The ground plan of the settings suggested a diamond-shape, as though one saw the "ring" from a dynamic corner view. Of course this conception could not be merely schematic. It worked properly because it was adapted to the content, style and meaning of the play.**
>
> ***Mordecai Gorelik*[4]**

Gorelik's boxing-ring metaphor involved no visual description, but used the dynamics of the boxing ring so that the play's conflicts were realized "as if" the combatants were in the ring. Gorelik's term "as if" is an important one, implying the opposite of description and demonstration. It is very doubtful that anyone who saw the Group Theatre's production of *Golden Boy* was aware of the boxing-ring image, but because of unconscious emotional association suggested by "sparring" dialogue, "ring" movements, and boutlike scenes, the audiences probably received a heightened sense of the play's conflicts.

Another production of *Golden Boy*—by an American collegiate-community theatre—used a projection of a famous prize-ring painting as a permanent scenic background for the play. The scene shown is the same one analyzed on pages 69–71.

5

That the painting is too well known to integrate fully into the production is one possible objection. But more important is that this treatment tells the audience the image instead of enacting it. And "as if" in a boxing ring does not mean *literally in* a boxing ring. Here the painter's image overpowers the playwright's and one can see that a metaphor illustrated is no longer a metaphor.

A Swedish production of exactly the same scene treated the problem quite differently:

6

In this case the sound of cars and music, which is supposed to under-ride the scene, seems more plausible than in the previous example, but the great scenic emphasis on the tourist's picture-postcard view of "The Empire City" upstages the playwright's simple love scene, thus offering an example of unnecessary illustrative naturalism similar to pictorial settings of the late nineteenth century.

Just as the boxing picture turns Gorelik's metaphor into illustration, so the use of forms and objects drawn from studies like Freud's essays on dream symbolism may result in productions which depend for their effect on the audience's intellectual interpretation of the forms employed, rather than on the enactment of a dramatic image. The result is a kind of footnoting—the "symbols" in the production acting as emblems or signs proclaiming the intended meaning to those in the audience who know the necessary references.

DOES THE PRODUCTION DISTORT THE PROPORTIONS OF THE PLAYWRIGHT'S IMAGE?

Since the play, like all works of art, is a rhythmic structure, any good interpretation of a play will respect its rhythms and proportions as a crucial aspect of the commanding image; any interpretative idea which distorts the rhythmic pattern of the play will be rejected as destructive of the play's meaning.

Often, of course, the ways in which a performance design has changed the play's proportions are not at all obvious. For instance, many productions of *Richard III* make spectacular use of the coronation ritual in Act IV, scene 2. It seems only good theatre sense to exploit this pomp, for the ritual, with all its display and processions, is in itself dramatic; however, a careful look at the text shows, suprisingly enough, that there is no coronation scene. True, Richard enters "in pomp," but he has already been crowned offstage; typically, Shakespeare has chosen to dwell on the effect of the event—Richard's behavior on the throne—rather than on the ceremony. Richard's murderous and arrogant nature is now free to do its worst; we see him plan the murder of the princes and then turn viciously on his coconspirator, the Duke of Buckingham. With this as the purpose of the scene, all the playwright needs is to establish the idea of royal splendor and power at the beginning as a frame of reference for the more important character revelations of the scene. To use anything more elaborate than an entrance "in pomp" is to throw the scene out of proportion and dilute the impact of the scene that follows.

The 1953 production at Stratford, Ontario, took no more time establishing royal splendor than the script implies. Preceded by a fanfare and members of the court who turned to await his entrance, Richard emerged from up center. Attached to his shoulders was a heavy ermine-trimmed cape borne by pages. As the King limped roguishly downstage, there seemed to be no end to the cape; gathered together by the pages so that it could pass through the door, it did not end until the King had reached the extreme front of the forestage—a distance of perhaps 20 feet. On a final flourish of music, the pages parted, ran to opposite sides of the stage, spreading and releasing the massive train with a billowing snap, so that in an instant, Richard and his costume had taken possession of the stage, covering it with a sea of red velvet. Pomp and excitement there was, but it was over in a matter of seconds, and served only as a properly brisk prelude to this character-focused scene. The rhythm of the script had been left intact, yet the meaning of the scene had been spectacularly enlivened.

The destruction of the rhythmic proportions in plays is especially noticeable in screen versions, probably due to theories of film art which insist that movies are necessarily more "visual" than stage plays. This leads film makers to think that to make a good movie interpretation they must: act out all offstage scenes even hinted at in the play, use as many different locations as possible by breaking up scenes into shorter sequences, and insert additional pictures between the lines of the play with as many cinematic effects as they can introduce to compensate for the fact that the play will not allow them to make a "pure" film. Extended discussion of filmed plays is included in Part Four, but here a few brief examples are enough to show the problem of distorted proportion:

Like the overinflated coronations in productions of *Richard III,* Max Reinhardt's reunion ballet for Oberon and Titania in *A Midsummer Night's Dream* stops the plot for several long minutes to introduce an elaborate parade ending in a sensual *pas de deux* all choreographed in the Ballet Russe manner by Mme. Nijinskaya.

The Hollywood version of *Romeo and Juliet* includes a double parade in its drawn-out treatment of Shakespeare's brief opening scene; before the dialogue officially begins, bystanders, in elaborate stage whispers, point out and name the two rival families.

> **In the Russian film of *Twelfth Night* (1956) much film is spent following Viola as she gallops back and forth between the houses of Orsino and Olivia, with no visible purpose beyond exhibiting the lady's horsemanship.**
>
> **Olivier sets off a cinematic and orchestral explosion along with the words ". . . perchance to dream" in his filming of the "To Be or Not To Be" soliloquy—the camera zooms in and out of focus as the violins scream; Hamlet's dagger plummets far down into the surf below, after which the speech quietly continues, "Aye, there's the rub. . . ."—Hamlet has changed his mind.**

Shakespeare's plays are not the only ones to have been thrown out of proportion by film productions. The movie of *Death of a Salesman* contains examples of settings changed merely for the sake of variety, as when Willy and family take a subway ride to Ebbets Field, and one classic example of a sequence both changed in setting and bloated for the sake of cinematic effect: On stage, Willy makes up his mind to commit suicide in a scene with his brother Ben, after which he leaves the stage and we hear his car start up and roar away; in the film, the end of the scene with Ben is played in the car while driving, so that the scene must end with the anticlimactic "excitement" of the typical Hollywood car-crash sequence—blurred lights flashing by intercut and/or double-exposed with close-ups of the driver's face, tilted camera careening through streets, and so on.

Good screen versions, even if they do increase the number of settings, tend to stick closely to the rhythms and emphases of the original plays. There are many radical differences between the media of stage and screen, but the rhythm at which a particular action must develop to be dramatic is not one of them.

In plays as in films, a good question for the critic to ask is: Is what is gained by the effect proportionate to the performance time consumed in its execution?

Just as too much or too little emphasis on some scenes or small errors in timing left uncorrected by the director may disturb the play's rhythm in time, so, too, mistaken or careless interpretations can result in serious distortions of the play's rhythmic proportions in space—distortions of the impact of its visual form.

For example, in answering the question "What is the play like?" the interpreter may quite justifiably decide that the "feel" of *As You Like It* implies certain spatial patterns which are quite different from the spatial patterns implied in the "feel" of *King Lear.* The interpreter may then go on to design settings which embody the patterns he has felt for each play. This reasoning seems sensitive and plausible, but it does not take into account the extent to which these plays include scenery in their commanding images. For both *King Lear* and *As You Like It* were written for the same acting space: a "Globe" stage—an open platform on which scenery played a minor role.

In other words, the original images of these plays were formed in terms of the characters, not of the environment —the play's visual forms, their spatial metaphors, are made of characters in motion, not scenic forms. Hence, in such plays, the more emphasis placed on the settings, the more risk there is of destroying the playwright's idea. Everyone acknowledges that this kind of destructive staging took place in the productions of Henry Irving, Beerbohm Tree, David Belasco, and others in their tradition, but it can and does happen with settings in modern styles. Shakespeare "spectaculars," from David Garrick to the Hallmark TV productions, are vastly out of proportion as interpretations.

Again, it is not only in Shakespearean productions that the interpreters must be concerned with these problems; the scenic proportions of the original image are important in modern plays as well. The form of plays like *Our Town, Death of a Salesman,* and *J. B.* are most intimately tied to their original use of the stage.

As pointed out earlier, a playwright often makes his stage a part of his image; if so, any new interpretation (and a film is necessarily a new interpretation) must deal with his stage to the extent that it is part of the play's image. In the cases of *Our Town* and *Death of a Salesman* we have film versions which offer interesting illustrations of the ways in which the original images depended on special uses of the stage which where not translated to the film medium, thus resulting in serious distortion.

It is debatable whether a valid film translation of *Our Town* is possible. Opinion on this hinges largely on whether one feels the author's conception of the play as "sceneryless" is only a stunt or an important part of the play's image. Various stage productions have used scenery in varying amounts, indicating a body of opinion that regards the original as just a novelty; however, one can argue very strongly that the play's universality is greatly aided by the absence of any scenic element that localizes and particularizes it. One can change a few place names and locate the play in almost any rural community in the Western world, and in many communities elsewhere.

The film version, by photographing a concretely real town, has narrowed the playwright's image from a play whose individual characters stand for the generations of man to a Hollywood story about "jest plain folks" in a particular New England town.

The fact that *Our Town* is made up of stage-bound

images incompatible with the cinema seems rather obvious; on the other hand, *Death of a Salesman* would seem to fit easily into a film treatment. Yet, Arthur Miller considered the film version a failure, and attributed the failure primarily to essential aspects of the play's form which could not be transferred to the film medium. Strangely, it was the apparently cinematic "flashbacks" of the play which proved unworkable for the film. As Miller points out:

> There are no flashbacks in this play but only a mobile currency of past and present. . . . The film version failed because the dramatic tension of Willy's memories was destroyed by transferring him, literally, to the locales he had only imagined in the play. There is an inevitable horror in the spectacle of the man losing consciousness of his immediate surroundings to the point where he engages in conversations with unseen persons. The horror is lost . . . when the context actually becomes his imagined world. . . . The setting on the stage was never shifted, despite the many changes in locale, for the precise reason that, quite simply, the mere fact that a man forgets where he is does not mean that he has really moved. Indeed, his terror springs from his never-lost awareness of time and place.[7]

In the film the literalism of the memory sequences makes Willy seem *insane* rather than trapped by his problems; the impression created is that he is having pathologically detailed hallucinations rather than simply forgetting where he is. The conventions and limitations of the living stage allow us to see these incidents for what they really are: "imaginary confrontations . . . tension between now and then"—part of Willy's reexamination of his life, which is a major part of the play's action, and which therefore at all costs must not be distorted.

Thus, in judging how well the production is executed, how well the rhythmic structure of the image has been articulated, the critic must be aware that every aspect of the performance: line reading and movement; costume and property details; the color and form of scenery and lighting; the shape and use of the acting space—everything that the audience hears, sees, and feels—is combined in a rhythmically proportioned pattern determined by the play's commanding image.

IS THE PRODUCTION PRECIOUS?

Preciousness and image making for the sake of making images are the greatest dangers involved in the use of the metaphoric approach described in this book.

From Meyerhold's 1910 production of *Don Juan*—with "Blackamoors inundating the stage with intoxicating perfumes, which flow drop by drop from a crystal flask onto a red-hot plate"—to next year's progressive jazz version of *King Lear,* the whole history of modern production design is stuffed with productions: oversceneried or stripped-to-the-bare-brick-walls; in silks and satins or in denim coveralls; in mauve, cerise, champagne; in black and white except for one red rose; on stages framed and unframed, singular and multiple, central and peripheral—all "new," "original," "daring," "experimental"—*and most of them, unhappily, conceived in terms of images.* For, finding an image through which to develop a production becomes all too easily an exercise in being inventive and "poetic" for its own sake.

For example, the perfectly valid image of the title property in *The Glass Menagerie*—"a miraculous ice-crystal palace in a smouldering dump"—in the hands of an over-enthusiastic image-making designer is apt to result in a marvelous abomination:

> **Enchantingly high . . . perhaps seven or eight feet; the iron-wire frame delicately wrought into a snowflake tracery hoar-frosted with sequins; shelves of ice-blue-tinted antique mirror-glass, their polygonal edges exquisitely icicled with multi-sized crystal prisms . . . the whole mysterious structure softly swaying from invisible wires that suspend it—a wintry chandelier—in the center of the hot, glowing-walled dirty oven of a room.**

Thus, an image which helps to clarify the dramatic function of this object can be turned into a Ziegfield Follies decoration which would destroy the play.

The many examples which might be cited of its misuse still do not invalidate the metaphoric way of working, but they make obvious the urgent need for the strictest self-discipline on the part of the interpreters and for merciless analysis and exposure of affectation by the critics.

To summarize, the following are the questions which, in variations adapted to each particular production, concern the critic interested in evaluating a production's total conception:

What was the playwright's intent?

> **Which is to ask, What is the total performance effect implied in the playscript? What is the commanding image?**

How was this intent communicated to his audience?

Which is really a further analysis of the precise shape and content of the image (see pages 49–53).

How does this new production communicate the playwright's intent to his new audience? Is it a good translation?

What are the interpreters trying to do?

Does the production create an image? Is it among the limited number of possible "right" interpretations? Or has the play been used to create a completely new image?

Does the production's form seem to have grown organically out of the play, or to have been imposed upon it?

Does the production suffer from illustration—or from distortion in time or space?

Is it self-consciously arty or precious?

How well do they do it?

Is the performance execution adequate to the demands of the concept? Is the production's image brought to life? Did the production communicate the image to the audience?

Was it worth doing?

Is the production worthy of serious attention? Was the audience's time in the theatre well spent? In the case of radical image making, is the new image as important an experience as one closer to the original might be? Is it as good?

PART FOUR: A Gallery of Production Interpretations

It is time to notice that nowhere in this discussion has it been said that even the most brilliant application of these ideas will produce the One Absolutely Right Interpretation. We can narrow down our discovery of purpose to a very limited, plausible range of rightness, and therefore be in a position to see what interpretations are marginal or wrong—but the area of valid interpretations remains a range, not a pinpoint.

What remains to be presented is the ultimate testing of these ideas. This can only be done by looking at some actual productions in detail, to see finally what is meant by a plausible range of rightness.

In this section, a series of case studies is used for two main purposes: to illustrate more completely the practical application of the principles previously presented, and to provide a record of what certain important and stimulating productions were like.

There are too few places where a person interested in a specific production can find any sort of satisfactory record of it. Details of even the most impressive productions we have seen fade from memory, and those we have not seen hardly exist for us at all. Even in this day of film and tape recording, the essence of a theatrical experience is maddeningly difficult to preserve, as Tyrone Guthrie's *Oedipus* illustrates later in this section. Yet it is important that the attempt be made to record not only the facts of the production, but the effects it produced, for without such records nothing like a continuity of artistic growth can be assured in the theatre.

Painters and sculptors can return to, and examine at leisure, the accomplishments and failures of earlier days; those who refuse to do so shut themselves off from an important kind of inspiration and are doomed to waste time repeating experiments already done. How much truer this is in the theatre, where it is vastly more difficult to re-create the production experiments of the past—a situation aggravated by the death of a truly pervasive repertory system, where young actors could learn from older players of brilliant readings and movement invented in the past. There remain, of course, the Comédie Française and some younger theatres in the same great tradition, where business, properties, prompt books, and sometimes whole productions are preserved for generations, and such publications as the *Variorum Shakespeare* in which certain staging ideas are collated or occasional books like Rosamond Gilder's record of John Gielgud's *Hamlet*—but in general the salvaging of production creativity for future study is only fitfully attempted.

One of the reasons that production records are rarely kept is that many theatre artists, and some of our finest ones, are hostile to the idea of drawing inspiration from models, and even prefer that their own accomplishments be "writ on water." Such fear of learning from the past seems to be a twentieth-century phenomenon—with at least one notable exception: Bertolt Brecht, who freely admitted the many sources he drew on for inspiration, and who left elaborate records of his own work.

Being a director as well as a maker of plays, Brecht was doubly conscious of the need to preserve the total intention of his work. He therefore created what he called "models" for the purpose of guiding future productions, leaving not only detailed prompt scripts and production notes, but also hundreds of photographs on individual productions, recording the changing groupings of the characters and many technical details. This man, whom no one will accuse of being uncreative, rejected the modern cult of originality and ridiculed the idea that such models would necessarily stifle the creativity of future producers: "We must free ourselves from the present contempt for copying. It is not the "easier" thing. It is not a shame but an art. . . . Give me a reasonable Model of *King Lear* and I will delight in building according to it."[1]

If we are after better and better productions rather than merely new ones, Brecht's position makes practical sense. If one of David Garrick's readings clarifies the meaning of a speech in *Hamlet,* why not use it? If we use Garrick, why not Gielgud, Olivier, or Scofield? Why not, indeed, copy the best of all four, building more interesting new productions out of the richness of earlier ones?

All of which gives ample reason (in addition to its primary value as illustration) for the assembling of this gallery of production concepts.

ANGEL STREET

This first case study raises no controversial issues, but illustrates very well the practical help which an image can give to the planning of a production. As in the case of *Born Yesterday,* discussed in Part Two, the fact that *Angel Street*

A scene from *Angel Street*.

2

represents the highly commercial genre of Broadway, and that it was produced by hardheaded practical men of the theatre, makes it an ideal reminder of this important point: *the usefulness of these working methods is not limited to classic, "artistic," or esoteric plays.*

The following article on the planning of the original Broadway production of *Angel Street,* written by the director Shepard Traub, is reprinted from the June 1942 issue of *Theatre Arts.* The commanding image of this play creates a feeling of imminent and mysterious mortal danger from which escape is unlikely, but possible. It should be noticed that while much of the production concept is directly engaged in this feeling, the initial idea is complimentary to the central image, rather than identical with it.

Patrick Hamilton's *Angel Street,* the surprise hit of the Broadway season, is unique in many ways. It won immediate success although it opened cold in New York without any of the usual fanfare. It is, besides, a thriller and, as such the first recent play of its kind to have delivered so rich a cargo of acclaim. Further, it is a play that requires only one set and five actors, seeming to involve only a minimum of production effort and cost. Yet, actually, it is the production technique, derived in large part from film methods and procedures, that makes *Angel Street* significant.

Whatever the "frontoffice" deficiencies of making motion pictures in Hollywood, and they are manifold, the director does enjoy the collective efficiency of technicians who work with him intimately *before* as well as during actual production. Once the shooting manuscript has been completed, every department concerned with the picture consults with the director, the art designer, research chief, costume designer, cameraman, property man, cutter, musical director and composer, electrician, location chief, assistant director. With these aids the director has worked out a detailed blueprint of the production before the camera starts rolling. Everyone knows what is expected of him, and follows through according to plan.

This is not the traditional policy of the Broadway theatre, but the production of *Angel Street* was predicated on precisely that basis.

For those who have not seen or read the play, it should be established that most of its action is performed with never more than two actors on stage; that condition gave me the key to a technique for the production. I resolved to approach each problem of staging just as if I were *photographing* the action. As a result, almost everything in *Angel Street* is played in what Hollywood terms "big head" closeups, or close "two shots," bringing the audience into intimate proximity with the actors.

The production staff of *Angel Street* comprised Abe Feder, lighting, Lemuel Ayers, designer, and Arthur Ebbetts, stage manager. Before anything was put on paper, we spent several weeks in consultation arguing theory and techniques, challenging each other's ideas, constantly applying the pragmatic test of what these ideas would mean to an audience in terms of suspense, humor, dramatic surprise. Not until there was absolute agreement did we go ahead with the business of constructing a physical production.

Perhaps the most effective way to analyze the production technique of *Angel Street* is to narrate the specific steps in these discussions aimed at fusing the best elements of motion pictures and the stage.

1. Our initial discussions centered around a ceiling piece. We accepted the premise of a "low camera" shooting up at the actors from the point of view of a theatre audience and decided that the ceiling was to be a prominent item in the set. A heavy beamed ceiling was much too costly so we substituted a richly painted canvas ceiling with an all-over rococo design. It was decided that the ceiling

would be pitched at a raked angle calculated to force an audience unconsciously back in its seats in order to study it. The parallel for such a ceiling effect may be discovered in *Citizen Kane* where the use of low camera setup made it necessary. The ceiling piece in *Angel Street* was evolved with another effect in mind; it was intended also to serve as a dead weight bearing down on the head of the chief feminine protagonist, who is haunted by the fear of unknown activity in the house on the floor above her. In connection with this ceiling piece we decided to construct a set that would be only 13 feet high instead of the conventional 14 or 15, to center the attention of our audience within a restricted "frame."

2. The height of the set quickly brought our attention to the question of depth. Most stage sets range in depth from 15 to 20 feet to give actors plenty of room to move around. The set for *Angel Street* was deliberately arranged to allow for only 13 feet in depth, since we wished to *confine* the actors and keep them down-stage, virtually in the laps of our audience. Since the action was to work *across* stage, rather than up and down (in order to keep it in the foreground), it was necessary to divide the stage in three general sections, stage left, centre and right, for three general groupings of the stage furniture—a couch, a table and two chairs, and a desk.

3. It was clear that difficult lighting problems would have to be faced and solved for such shallow acting areas. Feder decided to use only a minimum of "front pipe" lighting, with his principal light sources coming from the wings, off "boomerang" stands, and from the sides of the orchestra floor. Other concentrated lighting effects were achieved by shooting up from the footlights with strategically placed spots, and from the sides of the set through apertures, con-

cealed from audience view by pieces of bric-a-brac. Feder evolved the effect of motion picture "back lighting" by "cheating" spots from the top of our staircase *behind* the actors.

4. Mr. Hamilton in his manuscript referred to a staircase *off stage.* We decided to bring the staircase on stage, even though it was not correct tectonics for a Victorian room. (We rationalized that by assuming that the house was pre-Victorian!) Lemuel Ayers developed the notion of giving the line of the staircase a sharp upward thrust so that it would seem to ascend indefinitely into space. Feder complemented that with the decision to use light on the staircase arbitrarily, to flood it at moments when we wanted our audience to believe that someone was about to appear on the staircase and, conversely, to plunge it into darkness when someone did appear. On Hollywood sound stages, the intensity of light on a set is arbitrarily controlled by a rheostat and varied in relation to the position of the camera. For instance, when the camera pans over a given area of a motion picture set, if the action is to be heightened in effect for the lens, light is arbitrarily intensified or perhaps lowered in key. That principle is applied effectively and dramatically to *Angel Street,* bringing menace and suspense into the performance. When Judith Evelyn finally comes down the steps in the third act, she is modelled in a glow of light that makes her seem almost like an apparition.

5. To give color importance in relation to light and composition, most of the wall surface was made of a deep-blue velour with a detailed stencil pattern. The velour refracted light and compensated for the actual shallowness of the set so that our audience would not feel cramped by it. A vivid Victorian red was used effectively in drap-

eries and seat-covers, with dead-white statuary and somnolescent, green ferns for contrast.

6. For architectural motif we chose the neo-Gothic line, as correct for the Victorian period, to give a haunting, sinister mood. The Gothic arches and curves repeated in the fireplace, the staircase, over the door and window, and even in several chairs give the effect of daggers everywhere looming down, whether consciously noted or not.

7. To set the mood of the play and win the attention of the audience immediately, we decided to use a familiar but effective device before the rise of the first and third act curtains, the sound of rich, sonorous chimes like those of London's "Big Ben."

8. In motion pictures, a heightened effect is obtained by bringing the subject close to the camera. In the theatre, the normal convention is the reverse, to gain emphasis by sending the actor upstage, or what would correspond to away from the camera. For *Angel Street's* foreground composition I decided to bring my furniture relatively close to the footlights and to crowd it. In addition, the furniture was arranged to allow for "camera angles", placing the audience in the position of the camera.

With each detail in the production of *Angel Street* carefully plotted in advance so that we understood its function, the rest was simple execution. When it was finished, it was "hung" and mounted in exactly five hours, many hours under what most productions require. Two dress reheasals sufficed to achieve mechanical slickness, since we all knew in advance what we were after.

At the first rehearsal, the cast was shown a detailed model of the set and permitted to study it until they had a clear visual image of what the production would look

> **like. Having accomplished that, we settled down to the job of constructing a performance.**
>
> **The creation of special "business" for the play may be assigned to the department of pure theatre; the movement and composition of *Angel Street,* however, are almost completely derived from the Hollywood sound stages. There is scarcely a moment when a camera might not be following the action and recording it capably for a motion picture. There are the equivalents of high camera and low camera shots, over-shoulder closeups, tight "two-shots." Whenever an actor is in movement, a camera might be panning with him, dollying in slowly, or trucking back fast. The "frame" for the audience is almost entirely similar to that which is photographed on 35mm film. The dynamic movement that results gives *Angel Street* its special impact. . . .**

Many of the same effects might have been arrived at through other images; the oppressive threat of the ceiling, the shallowness and confinement of the setting, and the melodramatic use of lighting did not have to come from the metaphor of cinema—but the particular device used is less important than having some image that will work, and in this case the device certainly worked well.

The execution of this production concept illustrates many of the specific practices discussed earlier in this book. For instance, analogy to another art form was the basis for the production image. Once this had been recognized as a useful form-giving idea, all production notions were tested against it, and its unifying principle in effect selected or rejected interpretative proposals. It is interesting to note that rather than act as an alliance of independently creative artists, this producing group chose to operate by "absolute agreement" to a concept which indicated precisely what kind of thing each one of them had to invent. Also, while the movie image introduced elements such as the ceiling, it was association with the emotional effects of another art form—architecture—which gave the ceiling and some of the other elements their final form. And through all this, effect desired, rather than realistic accuracy, marked the dominant approach to this completely realistic play.

Most interesting of all is the thoroughness with which this production concept commanded the "design" of everything from acting to lighting. Analogy to the movie close-up determined the basic requirements of the floor plan; this in turn dictated the quantity, kind, and "camera angle" placement of furniture, and hence prescribed to an important extent what the actors could do. Even basic decor was determined by the closeup function, since the shallowness of the set was compensated for by dark blue velour wall surfaces, creating a virtual depth far greater than the actual one. The floor plan also generated the particulars of the lighting more markedly than is common; the plan accounted for the preponderance of side lighting and the emphasis on unusual placement of instruments. The lighting plot in turn selected some of the set dressing, making use of Victorian bric-a-brac to conceal its specially placed spots.

Since the show was hung in record time and the often grim problems of dress rehearsals were reduced to merely perfunctory ones, let it be said, finally, that besides the aesthetic ones, great practical advantages were the reward of this approach to *Angel Street.*

THE HOPKINS-JONES HAMLET: A PRODUCTION CONCEPT AND CRITICAL REACTIONS, 1922

The experience of Arthur Hopkins and Robert Edmond Jones in introducing New York audiences to "the New Stagecraft" in the nineteen-twenties raises provocative questions about the conflict between the audience's demand for easy communication and the creative artist's desire to experiment with new forms of expression. As a case study in the problem of translation, the famous Hopkins-Jones *Hamlet* illustrates several of the principal questions relating to production concepts that must concern the critic. For this reason the pertinent sections of several lengthy reviews, articles, and letters-to-the-editor are placed in a special appendix to this book. These writings are appended for other reasons: as examples of the unusual quality of the dramatic criticism to be found in the newspapers of this exciting period of American theatre—and most important for the discussion which follows, because the perspective of almost half a century of "New Stagecraft" now permits a reevaluation of this historic and controversial production, a reevaluation with special significance for present-day experimenters.

In the glow of nostalgic reminiscence about John Barrymore's spectacular success as Hamlet in 1922, it has been largely forgotten that this production by Arthur Hopkins and Robert Edmond Jones—one of a series of collaborations between the producer-director and the brilliant young scene designer—created a sizzling controversy. The debate centered on Jones's settings and the staging they were created to support.

Today, R. E. Jones is justly revered as the father of modern American scene design, and the quality of its designers is one of the important distinctions of the American theatre. Thus, Jones, as teacher, exemplar, and inspirer of many of our designers, has become a figure of almost legendary greatness. Readers of most of the books and articles about Jones's exalted position in our theatre can easily come away with the impression that "'twas ever thus" —though there are a few hints of his early struggles here and there. In actual fact, Jones's work in his pioneering period, when he designed some of his most experimental productions, inspired some critics with anything but reverence. The record of the Hopkins-Jones *Hamlet* reveals Jones in a phase of his career that is now but dimly remembered —as a hotly denounced avant-gardist.

Critical interest in the Hopkins-Jones *Hamlet* began building soon after the proposed production was announced. Their earlier production of *Macbeth,* featuring the often reproduced designs of daggerlike arches and overhanging masks, had created a great stir, and it is useful to consider it as a prelude to the *Hamlet* production. Stark Young, a staunch Jones partisan at the time, recalled the *Macbeth* in a note written in 1958, describing vividly its successful effect on him, but finishing with the comment:

> **If this production could have been put over with the public, it might have been a landmark in the history of the American theatre. As it turned out, the criticisms of it next day were only dull, abortive or aggressively stupid.[3]**

Robert Edmond Jones's design for *Macbeth:*

"Profoundly creative"? "Distinctly molar"? 4

The sort of reaction Stark Young and other supporters of New Stagecraft resented so much is indicated in this newspaper gossip column about the new production:

> A greater interest is accumulating in John Barrymore's "Hamlet" than has forerun any Shakespearean production . . . in the last twenty years. . . . The curiosity centers on . . . what manner has Robert Edmond Jones designed the Elsinore? . . . It may be guessed that Mr. Jones has not continued in the strain—the severe strain—in which he set the stage for Lionel Barrymore's "Macbeth." After the howl that went up on the first view of that distracting investiture, Mr. Jones was quoted as muttering that he would continue so to design the sets for Shakespeare's plays until the public should catch up with him, even if it killed Arthur Hopkins in the process. On the other hand . . . mingled in that howl, were a few acid remarks from John Barrymore himself. So it seems altogether unlikely that the new Elsinore will bear any resemblance to the distinctly molar Dunsinane which riveted the eye throughout the first act of "Macbeth," or that the Ghost of Hamlet's father, if, indeed, he is embodied on the stage at all, will seem kin at all to those three members of the Ku Klux Klan which danced around the cauldron in the witches' scene.[5]

On two counts, the columnist proved prophetic: Elsinore was not "molar," and the Ghost of Hamlet's father not only was not embodied, but became part of the noisy debate over the new interpretation. The production opened on November 16, 1922, and the first-night reviewers devoted much space to Barrymore's performance, but the settings came in for a good deal of comment in the first reviews and especially in later articles and letters. Stark Young's highly laudatory review probably verbalizes the intended effect of the production even more eloquently than Jones himself could have done it:

And I must admire the economy of business. . . . About all this production there were none of those accessories in invented business; there was . . . only that action proceeding from the inner necessity of the moment and leaning on life, not on stage expedients. . . .

It is in the scene where Hamlet catches the King praying and does not kill him . . . that the method of production employed by Mr. Hopkins and Mr. Jones is reduced . . . to its most characteristic terms. The King enters through the curtain, already used a number of times, with the Saints on it [this was one of the tapestry-like full-stage curtains that were drawn in front of the main unit set for several intimate scenes]. He kneels, facing the audience. He lifts his hands and speaks to heaven. Hamlet enters through the same curtain. . . . One man is here, one is there. Here are the uplifted hands, there the sword drawn. . . . Two bodies and their relation to each other, the words, the essential drama, the eternal content of the scene. No tricks, no plausible business, no palace chapel. And no tradition. A far more important end is sought. This production of *Hamlet* is important and is out of class with Shakespearean production from other sources . . . because it works toward the discovery of the essential and dramatic elements that from the day it was written have underlain the play. The usual Shakespeare production . . . goes in precisely the opposite direction. It does not reveal the essential so much as it dresses up the scene at every conceivable angle, with trappings, research, scenery, business. . . . Mr. Robert Edmond Jones has created a visual form that is for the most part—not always—inseparable from the thought of the play. . . . There is no clutter of costumes, no beguiling variety of apartments, but a rhythm of images, of light and shade innate to the moment, a pattern of figures with its own abstract truth.

> And all these, establishing as they do the line of the whole design, appear against that curtain with the saints, or in that hall with its beautiful spaces rising above the play of steps, its arch, and the moulding, high up, that conveys the subtlety of the planes. It is architecture at once austere and princely, lyrical and enduring. It has for me at least a quality of excitement in it like that of music; it seems not so much a setting as a rich shadow of thought behind the play's events. . . . [In its best passages, this production achieved] a fundamental pattern so simple and strong that it restored to the dramatic scene its primary truth and magnificence.[6]

Stark Young, as a proponent of the New Stagecraft, kept his review almost entirely positive—though he hinted at flaws—feeling, no doubt, that enough negative comments would be made by others. And they were.

The other critics, though they, too, found much to praise in this production, took care to pick out its faults, and some of the faults they found were precisely the things Stark Young had praised. Thus the *New York Sun* review, though it praised the set as "an ideal background for beautiful stage pictures," did so only after pointing out the faults of the production:

> Once more Robert Edmond Jones . . . endeavored to improve on Shakespeare. He has provided a very beautiful solid setting, an interior in the castle with wide steps in the rear center leading up to a high arched open doorway. . . . Such a setting created . . . uncertainty in the minds of the spectators as to how certain scenes would be managed. One of Mr. Jones's devices, which brought to mind the "Follies," . . . was to use a silk front drop and have the scenes played in front of it, thanks to an apron that had

> been built around the stage. Several scenes were managed by using other curtains that changed sufficiently the appearance of the stage. But the grave-digging scene proved an insurmountable difficulty and Ophelia's grave was dug inside of the castle, although the players and audience acted as though it was a graveyard. Naturally, the illusion was spoiled.[7]

Columnist Heywood Broun, who liked the production as a whole, was also disturbed by the burial: "Ophelia is buried in the front parlor. . . . The necessity of making a graveyard of the palace is not apparent . . ."[8] Jones's friend and colleague, Kenneth MacGowan, later defended the design as a "permanent architectural form" intended, like Shakespeare's stage, as a permanent, abstract part of the theatre, but even the loyal Stark Young had reacted to the set as an interior, calling it a "hall."

Many reviewers were profoundly disturbed by the very scene Young had chosen to typify the production:

> In the scene of the King at prayer . . . Claudius kneels on an apron over the orchestra pit holding his crucifix to the noses of the unfortunate fold in the front row. Hamlet enters through a curtain just behind him, draws his sword and then pauses to discuss with himself whether he will do murder . . . in tones audible to the last row in the balcony; yet Claudius, alive though he is to the danger of assassination and in terror of it, does not hear.[9]

John Corbin, drama critic of the *New York Times,* made these remarks in a long article in the Sunday drama section, in which he enumerated most of the objections that had been raised to the production, including a flickering projection

10

The Hopkins-Jones *Hamlet:* Burial of Ophelia and the Prayer Scene.

11

and an offstage voice for the Ghost (an innovation that met with so much disapproval that the traditional armored figure was put back into the production by the time it played Boston the next year). Corbin was most provoked by the large flight of steps leading to the arch upstage center, the most imposing element in the permanent setting. He felt that the design forced several scenes to be cramped downstage, and cited, with diagrams and dimensions, the Globe platform stage as the kind of performance space for which the action had been designed. Corbin took occasion to praise earlier experiments with Elizabethan-style staging of Shakespeare while condemning Jones for occupying the central playing area: "Mr. Jones's 'symbol' has usurped the area needful to the creation of any genuine dramatic effect. One cannot play Shakespeare up and down stairs."[12]

It was in reply to this article by Corbin that Kenneth Macgowan wrote a lengthy letter of defense, which was printed along with a reply by Corbin. Macgowan pointed out that the staircase actually did not take up most of the floor space, but only looked that way because of sight lines from the orchestra seats; he defended the staging of the prayer scene with the argument that Hamlet was not speaking aloud but speaking his thoughts in soliloquy, and further cited the work of Jessner and other continental directors to show that Shakespeare could be acted up and down stairs.[13] The wrangle went on for some time and generated considerable heat.

The fundamental criticism, shared by several objectors, was that a great play had been "sacrificed to the scenic whims of modern producers," as the *New York Evening Post* headlined a review by conservative critic J. Ranken Towse, one of the most vigorous objectors. But the fundamental complaint was tersely and wittily summed up in one of the many letters which appeared in the newspapers:

"Don't treat me as if I took your Robert Edmond Jones for a lilyhanded idler breathing mists," writes Virginia Tracy. . . . "Although quarreling with him," she continues, "automatically confesses me a Victorian, late, mid and early, I don't confess myself a slug, crawling. I can feel, just as if I were alive today, the vigor of Mr. Jones's creative imagination, the violence of its restraint, the beauty and force of its execution—perhaps it is with these I quarrel. For without them there would hardly be such a thudding crash of impact whenever he encounters that other not uncreative spirit . . . the author of the play.

Any Jones production of Shakespeare is to me a ringside where two gentlemen with a great deal to say enter into something like a life-and-death struggle to be heard, the one above the other. . . . In the bad old days of changeable scenery the most that Shakespeare had to contend with was a stuffy excess of prettiness and fussiness, so insignificant that one blast upon his bugle horn sent it to heel.

But now another poet challenges him to take the stage if he can, a poet vividly and most authoritatively intent upon quite a separate drama of his own—the drama of light and shadow, of line and mass, and all the romance and splendor and significance which he so intensely, so devotedly feels in these things that he is willing to put them over by whatever means comes to his hand, through even a play of Shakespeare, or any other medium having in it something that, by a little dexterity, he can wrench into their service. But alas! he cannot entirely stifle the writhings and mutterings of the drugged giant, bound hand and foot to be shaped, colored, clothed and nailed flat to the design of an artist believing in a world created out of repose, order, pure color, the most absolute simplicity, the absolute banishment of the detailed or the

> colloquial, a world above all statical, like the Arch of Trajan seen against a consistently night-sky. But does anyone really think that this is Shakespeare's world?[14]

After *Macbeth* and no doubt after *Hamlet*, R. E. Jones felt, with some anger, that the fault was with the audience—that they had not caught up with his ideas. This was in part true, for he had progressively less trouble of this sort as the years passed. Four decades of subsequent theatrical developments provide us, however, with a more complex and interestingly different view of the *Hamlet* controversy. The negative reviews remain surprisingly timely and forceful; many points continue to make excellent sense, and events since 1922 have given even greater significance to some reviews than they originally had.

Several of the most outspoken critics considered themselves open opponents of the New Stagecraft, making statements in the same spirit as the following one by J. Ranken Towse (though the others were usually less violent):

> [Arthur Hopkins] has become infected with some of the pernicious theories of Gordon Craig, and of what is called, by utter misnomer, the "new art of the theatre," which while comparatively innocuous in the case of modern exotic and abnormal drama, cannot be made to harmonize with the structure and spirit of those great classics in which the realistic and imaginative are combined in incomparable fashion. To attempt to modernize Shakespeare, to apply to his robust and soaring genius the finicking methods of a more artificial civilization is not only futile, but something worse than foolish. . . .[15]

But while these critics took a negative position, they nevertheless based their criticisms on the same principles that the New Stagecraft professed: organic unity of the performance and faithful interpretation of the author's intent. Thus, the views of *New York Times* critic John Corbin that:

> Any play of real merit . . . is an artistic unit, deftly articulated in all its members and rhythmically measured in its flow . . . rigidly subject to the laws of time and tone as a symphony.

and that

> Only by treating it with due regard to its inner structure, its implicit harmonies, is it possible to release its rhythmic energies and make them assert their sway upon the hearts and minds of an audience. . . .[16]

are in no way different, in the premises from which they flow, from the views of R. E. Jones as he expressed them three years later:

> In his mind's eye . . . [the designer] must see the high original intention of the dramatist, and follow it. . . . The designer's sole ambition must be to affirm and ennoble the art of these mystical Protagonists [the actors].[17]

Even when J. Ranken Towse damns the *Hamlet* production by saying:

> . . . the scenic scheme . . . expressly devised to simplify and expedite the action, did nothing of the sort, but . . . tended rather to delay and confuse it. . . . The acting, which ought to be the prime object of consideration . . . seems to have been considered . . . entirely subordinate to the scenery. . . .[18]

his critical standards are identical with Jones's and with those published only four years before this production by Arthur Hopkins:

> **Author, director, scene designer and actor must become completely the servants of the play. Each must resist every temptation to score personally. Each must make himself a free, *transparent* medium through which the whole flows freely and without obstruction.**[19]

It appears, then, that this controversy was not, as some of the participants assumed at the time, essentially a battle between advocates of stuffy "old-style" theatre and "mist-breathing, lily-handed" champions of "the new art of the theatre." Certainly the Hopkins-Jones *Hamlet* received its share of old-fogey reactions, but the main line of argument against it, which comes down to the fact that its production concept got in the way of the play, still seems a reasonable objection today and might indeed prove true for modern audiences.

The production concept for *Macbeth,* as Stark Young ruefully admitted, was a total failure; so, too, the concept for staging *Hamlet* was hardly an unqualified triumph of communicating Shakespeare, and consistently evoked strong objections. Why did the ideas of Jones and Hopkins not succeed in the manner they had hoped? Forty years of hindsight gives us some possible answers to this question.

It now appears that the scenic revolution called the New Stagecraft, far from being a total overthrow of the drama-smothering, opaque conventions of nineteenth-century production in favor of a new "transparent medium," actually succeded only in integrating and harmonizing the disparate elements of the performance—an impressive achievement, but one not as revolutionary as was thought at the time. Like the rebellion of a son who turns from the rigidly orthodox religion of his father to an equally doctrinaire atheism, the New Stagecraft was a change in outward form rather than in essential character. What had previously been quaint naturalistic detail or merely decorative displays of the scene painter's art, the New Stagecraft's directors and designers brought together and simplified into unified designs whose form expressed the aura of the play. But, judging from critical reactions in the case of the Hopkins-Jones Shakespearean revivals, the medium evidently remained opaque. In this case it retained too much of the tradition it was rebelling against.

The tradition, the essential character of both nineteenth-century staging and of the New Stagecraft, was pictorial, and this is strikingly revealed by these comments taken from both sides of the *Hamlet* controversy:

> **Seldom if ever, has a great play even in the days of Irving and Tree, been presented with a more richly spectacular background. The stage pictures were nobly designed and gorgeously brilliant or impressively sombre in color, while every grouping has been arranged with a view to pictorial effect.**
>
> ***J. Ranken Towse***

> **. . . that hall with its beautiful spaces rising above the play of steps, its arch, and the molding, high up, that conveys the sublety of the planes. It is architecture at once austere and princely, lyrical and enduring. . . .**
>
> ***Stark Young***

> **. . . like the Arch of Trajan seen against a consistently night sky.**
>
> ***Virginia Tracy***

In other words, the New Stagecraft was the final refinement of the picture frame theatre introduced by the architect-painters of the Renaissance. Under the influence of Gordon Craig,[20] and inspired by other European examples, Jones and Hopkins felt keenly the need to avoid merely picturesque or literal effects in mounting *Hamlet.* They aimed at designs that supported the play with a mood-evoking background rather than with illustrations of palaces and graveyards. But the solution was incomplete, for, as Tyrone Guthrie has put it, ". . . assuming that a satisfactory compromise can be reached in regard to scenery, a picture which is also not a picture, the problem still remains of how to relate the actors to their audience in the manner in which the author presupposed when he was writing."[21] The audience reactions to the Hopkins-Jones treatment of the prayer scene, one of the most often criticized aspects of the production, show that this production had not solved this problem. The audience was jarred by this breach of the proscenium-arch convention in a production which, however new in its concept, remained within the pictorial tradition.

And so we find that the "modernism" of Shakespearean production today, rather than supporting the avant-garde of 1922, has clearly endorsed the position of *New York Times* critic John Corbin, who cited experiments in the revival of the Elizabethan platform stage as the best way to produce the plays of Shakespeare and other classical authors. Though in appearance they are modern equivalents rather than archeological reproductions, theatres like the Chichester Festival Theatre in England; the Stratford, Ontario, Festival Theatre; the Tyrone Guthrie Theatre in Minneapolis and others—all follow what John Corbin called "the dramaturgic principle" of the Globe stage.

In sum, then, it is possible to place the New Stagecraft and one of its most famous examples, the Hopkins-Jones *Hamlet,* in a clearer historical light than has been formerly the case. The New Stagecraft, splendid as its achievements have been, appears to be simply the final sophistication of the pictorial tradition introduced to the stage by Italian court painters during the Renaissance. The *Hamlet* production, brilliantly executed in this tradition, nevertheless failed to be a "transparent" vehicle for the play as its creators had wished, and stands as an interesting example of a production concept somewhat at odds with what the playwright had in mind. In other words, the production idea was an incomplete answer to the question, "How does this production communicate the author's image to this particular audience?"

Noting this, one cannot help but begin to reevaluate some of the current enthusiasms in modes of staging. Will the many new "flexible" theatres—some of which seem to have been built by and for engineers—be used in the same old unconsciously pictorial-mechanistic vein? Or will the variable actor-audience relationships available in these theatres be used with the realization of the rich potential afforded by nonpictorial production concepts as represented most notably in the work of the Greeks and Elizabethans? Concerning matters of principle to be learned from this reevaluation, one suggests itself rather easily: It is the ancient, but once again modern idea that—as an interpreter of drama—the production-designing director is not fundamentally a painter or sculptor arranging human figures as parts of pictures; he is an actor with many bodies, performing a pattern of human action.

OEDIPUS: PLAY AND FILM

The Play

In 1954 at the Canadian Shakespeare Festival in Stratford, Ontario, *Oedipus Rex* was presented in the translation of Yeats. The open stage, the more than halfway encircling auditorium, its steep rake, even the rather general lighting —all would probably have seemed sufficiently "right" to Sophocles. The festival atmosphere of the production was also beautifully in accord with the circumstances for which the play was written. The elaborate civic-sponsored festival in the Athens of Sophocles' day could boast of drawing visitors from all over the Greek-speaking world, and so, too, could this Stratford festival claim to have attracted worldwide attention, even in its very first year.

In this, its second year, the electric excitement and justifiable Canadian pride was still running high. One could feel it in the daily shoptalk of the town, and at the theatre the opening ceremonies brought this feeling home with great force: first, a series of trumpet flourishes; then, in good Elizabethan tradition, a cannon roar reverberating through the bankside park to signal the performance; and finally, the audience standing, singing "God Save The Queen." This was no ordinary, dismissive nod to patriotic custom; the singing was strong, for through it—at once solemnly and enthusiastically—the intense local and national pride of Canada found a means of expression. This was clearly an important moment, perhaps one of the great cultural achievements of the English-speaking world, and even the Americans in the audience, for whom the melody also has such familiar emotional value, felt a privileged membership in this enterprise of high daring and merit. Thus, both in the wraparound seating and in audience spirit, this was a *community* festivity to a degree that plays no part in ordinary playgoing. And nothing could have been more favorable for the performance of this ancient play.

With the citizens of Canada now gathered comfortably about the playing space, the lights drain into a moment of expectant darkness, and then refill the bowl of the theatre to materialize the citizens of Thebes. They have somehow come from us, the surrounding crowd, and are converging on the forestage in the hope that Oedipus will appear. Many of the supplicants bear censers from which an astonishing pall of smoke boils up, hangs for a time like a veil . . . only to lift and reveal a shining figure, gold from foot to crown, entering from the permanent colonnade at the rear of the stage. This is Oedipus the King.

The chorus, all in masks, is costumed in earth colors, rough-textured, voluminous robes, which give them, individually and collectively, a shapeless anonymity. The masks are extreme stylizations of sorrowing and of peasant homeliness, and run strongly toward the grotesque. By contrast, the king stands out sharply, a burnished lamp among old rags. He is larger than life, his sandals are thicksoled, his fingers lengthened, his costume padded, and his head made massive by an all-enclosing mask. The crown is made of curving thin spikes—like thorns.

The chorus intones its lines in a half-sung, half-spoken manner; likewise, the delivery of Oedipus is formal recitation rather than conversational reaction.

Now Tieresias appears—a startling figure all in white. At first glance his mask seems to be that of a skull, bone white with gaping black sockets for eyes, but the nose is long and sharp, very beak-like. In fact, the fingers are talons; the feet, whenever one can glimpse them beneath the floor-length robe, are clothed in a suggestion of feathers and claws; and the long necklace is made of eggshells. Perhaps the birds of augury, which this prophet uses to foretell the future, have been the source of the costume image.

The ensuing scene becomes lively. The quality of incantation, so characteristic of the speaking up to this point, begins to diminish during the give and take of the violent argument between king and prophet. In his passion, the blind old seer mistakenly believes Oedipus to be standing opposite him, plunges in that direction, and topples from the stage, being saved only at the last second by the arms of the chorus. Worked up to an even greater pitch, he collapses and delivers his final "curse" from the floor, on his back, one arm pointing heavenward.

Creon and Jocasta too are enveloped in masks and costumes which exaggerate their proportions. The Queen is the color of slightly tarnished silver; Creon is bronze. After the argument with Creon, the cadenced, chant-like delivery becomes more prominent again, and the performance continues with its oddly detached atmosphere. Dimly, on the far side of the platform, one can see the audience, quiet, deeply absorbed.

As the tragedy develops, moments become more and more lyrical in treatment, and at one point, the chorus breaks into full song, singing a mournful lament for their king.

For his final scene, the blind Oedipus emerges from the palace in a thick, dark dull red robe. His head and shoulders are covered by a heavy black net, and the effect, while strange, is a powerful one. The scene with the children is also singular: they circle slowly around him, in a slow, funereal dance, while the lines are all but sung.

At the end, the nearly two thousand spectators sit spellbound for a few moments. Under the mood of this performance no one dares race for the exit before the curtain call.

22

***Oedipus* at Stratford, Canada.**

That the concept for this production of Oedipus was at least partly a ritual-based idea was clear in the performance. The cantorial delivery, the hymns, the symbolic veil of blindness—all contributed to the impression of a performed litany. And the director, Tyrone Guthrie, had written in more than one article that he saw Oedipus as a kind of Christ figure: the legendary Greek was a miracle-working savior of his people, had his own Gethsemane of agony and doubt, and his final self-sacrifice. Thus, the tragedy was to be performed like a mass, with the actors commemorating the sacrifice of Oedipus in ritual recitation, without trying to convince the audience that a real event was taking place. Now whatever one may think of this production, one thing needs pointing up as a frame of reference in evaluating it: this 2,000-year-old play was given a successful professional performance, one which consistently held large popular audiences, and judging from the final response, one which made a deep and moving impression. To this important extent, at least, it was an effective translation.

What remains to be asked is whether the idea that "this play is like a mass" was complimentary to the tragedy's commanding metaphor of light and darkness, and whether the image chosen was well executed.

The first question requires some thought about the playwright's intentions in terms of "religion." For the Greeks religion seems to have been radically different from anything we have been accustomed to since the Judaic-Christian tradition conquered Western Culture. In Greece priests had a role in life so minor that they are scarcely mentioned in the literature; there was no authoritarian church, no bible, and no rigid catechism embodying religious doctrine. The rigorous enjoyment of an athletic, singing, or theatre contest was for the Greeks an affirmation of the exciting forces at work in the universe, and hence these things were a form of religious expression. In thinking of Sophocles writing a mass-like play, it is well to recall that this playwright lived in a culture for which such expressions as "God loving" and "God fearing" simply did not exist, and at ceremonies where a priest did officiate, he did not even wear a specially distinctive costume. If the typical Athenian would not have agreed that "Man is the measure of all things," nevertheless he did not by any means represent the opposite, or spiritual, point of view. Thus, the enormous zest for occasions in which human accomplishment could be thrillingly realized—in contests especially, even contests in the writing of tragedy.

Consistent with this, the plays themselves, no matter how serious and spiritual, typically have for their climactic scenes vivid debating matches between two splendidly matched antagonists. The arguments between Oedipus and Tieresias, and again with Creon, are typical of the Greek love of human prowess exhibiting itself through public rivalry and contention. And it is precisely in such scenes that the Stratford production concept seemed not to fit the play.

In the big, head-on clashes, the performance eased out of its templelike tone into the here-and-now sound of good, hot argument—a quality which seems inherent in the way these scenes are written, despite their formal structure. This is not to say that the disparity in playing style was terribly distracting, but if, as this book contends, a good production image should work easily and consistently without requiring special adjustments, then this fluctuation between ceremony and real verbal conflict was symptomatic of something wrong. Nor was this the only thing about the interpretation which called itself into question.

As one might guess, when Tieresias nearly fell off the

stage and when he delivered a religious passage, an oracular revelation of doom, lying flat on his back—these things, coming as they did after a strong churchlike impression had been established—were jarring and distracting. Nor was it clear just why the truth-seeing blind man was so forcefully represented as a bird. The device was intriguing, but it made him seem less an awesome prophet than a spook. As it was performed it seemed to have little to do with the kind of religious ritual suggested by the preceding action.

To be sure, many elements of the production worked well for the play. Just as the radiance of Christ was symbolized in some medieval productions by overlaying the actor's face and hands with gold, Oedipus all in gold was a striking, effective device, and both the symbolism and fascinating unreality of this kind of costuming provided a dramatic yet ceremonial detachment which conveyed an exalted feeling of solemnity—certainly an appropriate emotion for this great tragedy. And the chanting, the hymns, some of the other symbolic devices such as the veil of blindness, these things keenly communicated the terrible dignity and seriousness of the script.

In sum, the analogy with Christian ritual seemed to bring to life crucial aspects of Sophocles' work but to need setting aside at certain moments, particularly in the big scenes whose excitement depends on direct human confrontation. One is tempted to say that therefore the image chosen, being only partly successful, was wrong. But one wonders what the effect would have been if the verbal duels had also been handled in a thoroughly ritualistic way. This would have given the performance greater consistency, though whether this kind of change would have resulted in a more accurate and dramatic translation of the tragedy is very much open to question.

As for how well the production concept was executed, the rather disturbing behaviour of Tieresias, his characterization as a supernatural man-bird, the fact that the Herdsman looked for all the world like a sheep—such things are hard to justify in terms of the analogy with ritual commemoration. It is interesting that in the program note for this production, written by the director, no mention was made of the ritual idea, but rather the entire discussion of meaning was concerned with pointing out the light-dark symbolism as a key to the play's nonliteral significance.

Since it is rather easy to find things in this production concept which suggest that it was not in sufficient harmony with the commanding image Sophocles used, one wonders why the live performances had the impressive effect which they so obviously did. This brings us back to the point made at the beginning—for undoubtedly a large part of the successful impact of this production lay in its close parallel with the community-centered assumptions of the original performance. In this area the playwright's idea of theatre and audience was realized to a degree which one has to have experienced by seeing the Stratford performances to appreciate fully. The festival spirit of the city, the audience's proud and deep sense of "family," the community-concept floor plan of the theatre—all these worked together in such measure as to make this particular effort to translate *Oedipus Rex* a quite memorable event. The same, unfortunately, cannot be said for the film which was made of this performance.

The Film Version

Produced by Leonid Kipnis, 1957;
directed by Tyrone Guthrie.

This film is an example of a photographed stage production which makes little attempt, other than the use of close-ups and varied camera angles, to change the theatrical character of the production. Since the stage production was in 1954 and this film was released in 1957, it was apparently made some time after the first staging of the play. It is interesting chiefly for what it documents of on-stage elements described above, and for what it proves about the importance of theatrical context in the evaluation of performances.

On stage Oedipus was first played by James Mason; in the film Douglas Campbell plays the role, and while this accounts for a number of differences, they are not the ones which need concern us here. The greatest difference, the crucial one, is that the film is utterly lacking in the very thing which helped to make the stage production a success —there is not one bit of the exciting sense of audience, of community, of the sheer presence of almost two thousand faces enveloping the players, tensely participating in the ceremonial commemoration of a great tragic event. One might object that a film version could scarely capture that, even if it tried, but whether it could or not, it does not, and that makes a terrible difference. The effect is as if one were to turn on the traditional television coverage of midnight mass on Christmas Eve and find that the congregation had been cleared out so that one or two cameras could work very close to the priests and altar boys, who would be conducting their ritual against a temporary neutral background for the sake of the program. The sense of an enormous, functioning church, alive with the murmur of hundreds of communicants would be lost in such a TV treatment, and the resulting chill would hardly render the mass meaningful, or even interesting. The *Oedipus* film seems to be a very similar case.

For the camera the tragedy is provided with a skillfully unobtrusive curving backdrop which does away with the architectural background present in the stage production. Since the camera never moves back for a really long shot, the feeling of distance presupposed by the playwright and by the director is also lost. The costumes, beautifully executed to register at fifty feet (the drapery, for example, being highlighted and shadowed with an airbrush), look uncomfortably stagy at four feet, and so do the masks. Tieresias particularly, at this close range, looks like something out of a horror movie, whereas on stage, he was merely a bit distractingly odd. It is probable that the lack of an audience, and the different demands of the microphone also produced some unwanted changes. Thus, while the film makers apparently intended no serious changes in the theatrical nature of this interpretation, the resulting change was in fact a drastic one, and, in the opinion of this evaluation, disastrous. It might even be said that what comes to the surface in this laudable attempt to preserve a memorable theatrical event are the very weaknesses which were pointed out in analyzing the live performance. The inconsistencies, the rather over-theatrical moments, all seem glaringly bad on the screen, when in fact they were not so on the stage. Again, Tieresias is the most notable example. On stage, his distracting tumble seemed due merely to his blindness and excitement; however, under the exaggerating eye of the camera his fall suggests an apoplectic fit. While this sort of thing provides a kind of momentary interest, the general consequence of the film—like the hypothetical TV Christmas mass—is a strange and dull translation of *Oedipus Rex*.

TROILUS AND CRESSIDA: TWO TRANSLATIONS

The relative character of good interpretation has been implied in much that has been said in this book: in an art mode where the medium constantly transforms itself—actors, audiences, stages all eternally changing—we have no choice but to think of the rightness of each production in terms of its effectiveness as a necessarily new translation.

This study of two productions of the same play offers an interesting contrast: an essentially similar concept in two variations conceived to meet the attitudes of differing audiences.

By 1601 English optimism over the defeat of the Spanish Armada had waned; Elizabeth I was nearing the end of her reign, and nearing it more like a crotchety tyrant than the "Gloriana" of a few years earlier. Vicious intrigue and corruption plagued the court as much as ever, and European enemies watched the English throne with malicious vigilance. It was at this time and in this atmosphere that Shakespeare wrote *Troilus and Cressida,* a bitter play about the Greeks and Trojans. The play is a biting, satirical treatment of the Homeric epic and its medieval versions. It ruthlessly exposes the maggots under the beauty of pomp, chivalry, and honor in love and war, and it has long been considered an unpleasant play. Until recently it has had almost no stage history, for its antiheroic, antiwar attitude confused and irritated the "love and honor" generations of the eighteenth and nineteenth centuries. But, by the 1930s war was again being viewed with horror and cynicism, and Shakespeare's peculiarly "modern" attitude toward it in *Troilus and Cressida* stimulated new productions. In a real sense, this play may be said to have been rediscovered for the stage in recent times.

Of the several modern productions two have been selected, both of which were produced in London, with similar objectives but eighteen years (one draft-age generation) apart; thus, they illustrate differences in audience attitudes of two postwar generations, creating two quite different translations.

In Modern Dress

In 1938 the play was produced in London in strictly contemporary dress. The production was discussed in *Theatre Arts Monthly* in December, 1938, as part of "The Scene in Europe."[23] The two pictures and all the quoted material which follow are from this article; Ashley Dukes makes the opening comment:

> ***Troilus and Cressida*** **must have gained something, in Shakespeare's own day, by its trick of presenting Elizabethan wit and poetry in Greek dress. It was, in fact, modern thought in costume. The producer today who resolves to give it in modern dress must be prepared to sacrifice this burlesque element of neo-classicism. He loses something, but whether he gains more the spectator of the modern-dress *Troilus* at the Westminster must judge for himself. It is delightfully mounted, and directed in the liveliest way by Michael Macowan. The Ulysses of Robert Speaight is a cultivated, globe-trotting gentleman of great subtlety. And if the disillusionment with love and war alike, which is the motive, comes over to the spectator chiefly as irritation, that is much more the fault of the poet than of any interpreters.**

Michael Macowan's 1938 *Troilus and Cressida:*

These lovers cry—Oh! Oh! they die!
Yet that which seems to wound to kill,
Doth turn oh! oh! to ha! ha! ha!
So dying love lives still. . . .

The modern-dress presentation of *Troilus and Cressida,* which Shakespeare appears to have written out of his own bitter disillusion with the two great obsessions of mankind, love and war, exactly at the moment when all Europe was teetering on the brink of struggle and destruction brought the Mask Theatre Company the approval of London critics. In their fresh settings lines usually dismissed as vague and incomplete took on alarmingly appropriate meanings, and the modernity of the piece was demonstrated by the ease with which Max Adrian could draw from the bitter text a fitting song for a sophisticated cocktail party.

Michael Macowan's 1938 *Troilus and Cressida:* Cressida leaves Troy:

I charge thee use her well, even for my charge;
For, by the dreadful Pluto, if thou dost not,
Though the great bulk Achilles be thy guard,
I'll cut thy throat.

In his satiric picture of the Trojan war and the carelessness with which an entire civilization is ruined for the sake of a light woman, Shakespeare turns out to be the author of a vehement antiwar drama. Dorothy L. Sayers is convinced that *Troilus and Cressida* 'is a play about war and not about a love affair. Modern-dress productions frequently have this merit of restoring the emphasis to the place where Shakespeare put it . . . but the thing that strikes one in even a cursory reading of this most difficult work is that here is the great "war-debunking" play, whose savage bitterness never has been equalled before or since.' The critic of *The Times* bears out Miss Sayers' belief by remarking that 'it is a play to blight any tender little shoots of illusion, especially about war, which may have dared to push out since the Treaty of Versailles was signed.'

After generations of popular distaste for *Troilus and Cressida,* both audiences and critics were startled by the timeliness of the play as revealed in this 1938 production, and both were generally warm in their approval of the performance. It would seem from this response that an effective translation of the work had been achieved. In the discussion of the 1956 production which follows, the view is taken that again an intelligent and reasonably accurate version was created.

In Edwardian Dress

What was effective and acceptable to the pre-World War II audiences of 1938 was no longer acceptable to the audiences of 1956. This is true not only in the attitudes toward war, but also in audience attitudes toward Shakespearean production. The "stripped-down" modernism of the 1938 production was appropriate to the taste of that period which in America saw Orson Welles' bare-stage *Julius Caesar,* Thornton Wilder's *Our Town,* and other antidecorative, antispectacle productions. In 1938 Tyrone Guthrie had directed Alec Guinness at the Old Vic in a modern-dress *Hamlet.* In 1956 for *Troilus and Cressida* Guthrie chose Edwardian dress and appropriate settings to suit new attitudes toward war, and made his production rich enough in color and pageantry to satisfy audiences which felt that pageantry is an essential part of Shakespearean production. The director and designer collaborated closely in working out a concept for mounting the production. The following note was written especially for this book by Frederick Crooke, the designer:

A production of *Troilus and Cressida* presented difficulties of presentation, for a modern audience, to a greater degree than many of Shakespeare's other plays. It is so "modern" in feeling that to dress it in the trappings of ancient Greece seemed to be both out of key and pedantic. The director, Tyrone Guthrie, suggested to me, at our first conference, that the theme of the futility of war, internal faction, and decadence might be brought home in a stronger measure to a modern audience if the "period" was moved nearer to our own day. To bring it right up-to-date appeared to be no better than to leave it in antiquity, since to glamorize war, and thus show it in its greater futility, could hardly be achieved by battle dress and antinuclear clothing.

Without being too specific, when could we "date" our play? When was the last time that war was waged, in its beginning at least, under the banners of righteousness, sacrifice, and glory? The First World War, perhaps, its excuse, the murder of an Austrian archduke, no more fundamentally important than the abduction of Helen! So, vaguely between 1910 and 1914 seemed to present a clue, at least for the costumes. Many in the audiences would remember nostalgically the hobble skirts and aigrettes of their youth and their escorts elegant in broad-striped trews and gold-frogged tunics, and going to war in "full-dress" appeared to be not such extreme artistic license when it is remembered that the French Poilu in August 1914 marched to defend the Marne dressed in a kepi, blue coat, and red trousers!

The setting provided another problem, as with all of Shakespeare's plays; the frequent change of locale could not be visually attempted, so that a permanent setting was the only answer.

After much discussion and many scribbles a symbolic idea was arrived at. Upstage center, a large "trophy" consisting of a cannon backed by a bloodred column surmounted by a gilded grenade, and flanked by large standards. Downstage, on either side, other decorative machines of war, on both sides of the apron stage flags, lances, muskets, and drums completed the warlike symbols. None of this paraphernalia attempted to represent a "realistic" conception of war but rather in a "toy soldier" way to suggest the glamour of war with its parade-ground pomp and chivalry. Since many of the scenes took place on the field of battle, in the Headquarters tents of the two protagonists, two huge curtains, one red and one blue, bearing the devices of "Troy" and " Greece" dipped in from either side downstage to provide a background for the Councils of War. There were two scenes, however, which demanded a certain intimacy, the Helen and Paris scene and Troilus and Cressida's "farewell." These we agreed could not be played against the generalized atmosphere of the setting. Two trucks were devised, one for the "Helen" scene, an Edwardian conservatory, its outrageous flippancy completed by a white and gold piano upon which Helen tinkled out Viennese tunes in the midst of hothouse plants. Cressida's house had to be more sombre, and an attempt to suggest *art nouveau* gave some sense of period. The final battle scenes were played on an almost bare stage and at the end, as the smoke of battle began to drift away, a cannon-shattered trophy provided a gaunt silhouette against a black-gold cloth.

26

(Opposite) Tyrone Guthrie's 1956 *Troilus and Cressida:* The Trojan Palace.

27

Tyrone Guthrie's 1956
Troilus and Cressida:
Departure of Hector.

28

Tyrone Guthrie's 1956
Troilus and Cressida:
Helen.

As for the uniforms, Greece tended to be based on a "Prussian" model with Ulysses as an admiral of the Grand Fleet and Agamemnon a bearded kaiser. The Trojans became "Life Guards" with all the dash of burnished helmets and breastplates, their tunics being either citron yellow or dove gray depending whether their regiment was the "guards" or the "blues."

The women's dresses, deriving from models of Worth, Paul Poiret, and Redfern, attempted to create the "Ascot" atmosphere of the Trojan court, its luxury and frivolity, without a care for the tragedy that awaited it.

Troilus and Cressida was one of the plays the Old Vic brought to New York in 1956, and the programs at the Winter Garden Theatre carried the following note by Tyrone Guthrie:

Troilus and Cressida have never quite established themselves like Romeo and Juliet or Tristan and Isolde. This is because their play is not a romantic but a satirical comedy. Troilus is rather a sensual, ordinary young fellow, brave and trustworthy, who just happens to be born a prince. Cressida—the evidence is overwhelming—is a minx.

The play's story is about two young lovers parted by the exigencies of war. It is also, and equally importantly, about a plan to arrange a single combat between Hector, the eldest son of the King of Troy, and some antagonist elected by the Greeks. In contemporary terms this is rather like suggesting a television debate between Shepilov and an antagonist chosen by the White House. Nobody thinks the single combat (or debate) can settle the issue; it is a matter of propaganda and prestige. Therefore, the election of the Greek protagonist presents a highly ticklish political and personal problem.

> **Enjoyment of almost any satirical work depends upon analogy with our own environment. Shakespeare sets his play at the time of the legendary siege of Troy by the Greeks. He derives his characters from Homer. But Shakespeare's Agamemnon, Ulysses and Nestor are not heroic; the feet of clay are exposed.**
>
> **The play's theme seems to us to be War and Lechery contrasted with War and Honor. We are shown two groups of people at war and how, under high tension, sexual conventions are ignored and civilized conceptions of honor become twisted and corrupted.**
>
> **The play is not presented in costumes or setting which suggest a Homeric period or environment. If we had dressed it in "classical" style, in togas and sandals, it would not be easy to differentiate instantly between soldiers and civilians, Trojans and Greeks. It would also be more difficult to show that these classical figures were being presented with some degree of mockery.**
>
> **Yet we did not feel that the play should be presented as completely "modern" for one single reason: one of its important premises is that war is sport, a premise to which no one nowadays can possibly subscribe. Therefore we have set the play back to a date when such a view was still widely held, but as near as possible to our own times: namely, just before 1914.** [29]

While such disparate critics as Kenneth Tynan and Claudia Cassidy liked the performance, in its American presentation the Old Vic production was criticized by some for losing Shakespeare in spectacular and farcical effects; in this connection, the following comment, from a letter to the authors from Dr. Guthrie, is worth noting:

> **Bear in mind that the American production suffered from the incurable disease of being in the Winter Garden Theatre, which is just fine for Ziegfield Follies, but absurdly too large for a difficult and subtle text. Broadly spectacular effects came off, but subtlety just flew out the window.**

Once again, the architecture of the theatre affected the meaning of a production by changing its emphasis in spite of the intent of the interpreters.

But even under these unfavorable conditions, many who saw the New York performances found the production excitingly meaningful in a way extremely rare among Shakespearean productions. The effect of the production was a startling feeling that the play had been written within the last three or four years by a great poet-dramatist contemporary with Bertolt Brecht rather than with Ben Jonson. Where other Shakespearean productions, even excellent ones, tend to include as part of their effect a feeling of "how interesting this old play turns out to be in the theatre," this production made one feel that the play was addressed directly to a modern audience.

One thing that set this production apart from other modernizations of Shakespeare was the way details of the production concept were made to strengthen the play's meaning; often, the choice of a particular period of costuming is merely a generalized decision "to get away from Elizabethan or Greek and Roman" and penetrates no further into the meaning of the production. This was not true here.

Early in the play (Act I, scene 2) a retreat is sounded and Shakespeare has Pandarus and Cressida chatter away about the passing soldiers as they stand on the walls of Troy to watch the warriors leave the field. In the Old Vic production these two shallow aristocrats stood on the apron of the stage, facing the audience, binoculars in hand, decked out as for the Ascot races, and yoo-hooed at the soldiers as if at favorite jockeys.The mood of war as sport was amusingly and disturbingly set.

The loud, grumbling entrance of a pre–World War I field photographer, complete with tripod, view camera, and flash powder, was amusing—but this apparently merely novel touch was quickly justified by its underlining of the bitter irony of the play. The first business of this photographer (Thersites) was to pose the Greek admirals in a satirically pompous photograph of their "historic" meeting, which waited for the flash before beginning its business. The original script scarcely bothers to explain the presence of Thersites, an apparently unoccupied civilian, at the scene of battle. But the presence of Thersites, the war photographer, seemed not only satisfyingly plausible, but his role as the cynical, uninvolved commentator was actually enhanced by the "war correspondent" impression. For example, when Thersites, in a later scene, entered cursing and grumbling, "Agamemnon—how if he had boils—full, all over, generally?" his photographer's role added bite to the intended sting by having him say the line as he viciously retouched a poster-sized enlargement of the Greek admiral.

The additional business, restricted to the early scenes, of the "spit and polish" aspects of military life was effective in making points about men playing at war: Playing scenes while reviewing the troops, officers punctuated their lines by absent-mindedly buttoning a stray button here, adjusting a strap there as they went down the line. The Trojan "Life Guards" uniforms, their polished breastplates gleaming, created a quite rich effect of the militarism of the recent past, though the ironic point that these were the uniforms at the "glorious" blunder of the "Charge of the Light Brigade" probably had more impact on British audiences than on American.

The dipping flags which formed a richly colored tent were particularly effective in one scene involving Achilles. Here, with Achilles in the Arab-like lounging robe (Lawrence of Arabia?) and Patroclus also "out of uniform," their dishabille contrasting strongly with the full-dress uniforms of the other Greeks, the scene had a flavor of late Victorian "oriental" decadence. In such an atmosphere, Thersites' line to Patroclus took on an incisiveness that might be missed in a more conventional mounting of the play: "Thou art thought to be Achilles' male varlet . . . , his masculine whore."

One of the most effective strokes came, appropriately, at the play's close. The war having broken out in earnest, Troilus having been betrayed, Hector foully murdered by Achilles and his minions, and the stage a smoke-filled shambles, Pandarus, still in Ascot gray coat and top hat, but now a war refugee, entered carrying his suitcase and sat down on it, center stage, to complain ironically about how bawds are treated in this world. His scene ends the play with a song, which in this production was set to a low-down blues tune recalling Kurt Weill's *Threepenny Opera* score. It was a fitting accompaniment to the "Brechtian" viciousness of Shakespeare's verse:

> **As many as be here of Pandar's hall,**
> **Your eyes, half-out, weep out at Pandar's fall.**
> **Or if you cannot weep, yet give some groans,**
> **Though not for me, yet for your aching bones.**

Brethren and sisters of the hold-door trade,
Some two months hence my will shall here be made.

. . . .

Till then I'll sweat and seek about for eases,
And at that time bequeath you my diseases.

Though one might feel inclined to carp at one or two farcical bits of business, this is far from agreeing with some voices that were raised to complain that "the poetry was lost." Perhaps it would be more accurate to say that in this production "the poetry was found," for its intended nastiness communicated with a shocking effect easy to miss in merely reading the script.

PETER BROOK'S KING LEAR

A tradition-shattering *King Lear* opened at Stratford-on Avon on November 6, 1962. Peter Brook's production, with Paul Scofield as Lear, astonished everyone, and is believed by some prominent critics and performers to have altered our conception of the play for all time to come. Within three months after the opening, this interpretation was not only a critical triumph, it was a "smash" at the box office, and tickets were even being sold on the black market. Articles were written asking that Europe and America be allowed to see the Royal Shakespeare Company in this most difficult of Shakespeare's plays, and the pleas were not ignored. After its London run, the Brook-Scofield *Lear* was seen in Paris where it won the Challenge du Théâtre des Nations and the Prix de la Jeune Critique. It then played in

West Berlin, Prague, Budapest, Bucharest, Warsaw, Helsinki, Leningrad, Moscow, and finally in America. A historic event in Western theatre.

That it was a startlingly new approach which was generally well received is reason enough for interest in it, but this interpretation is also one of those rare cases in which a single artistic authority guided every aspect of the production. Peter Brook directed the play; he also designed the lighting, costumes, and scenery. He is known as anything but a rigid formulist, preferring, along with his collaborators, to experiment and "work it out as he goes," but there can be no doubt that this *King Lear* was largely the conscious design of the director.

The moment one entered the auditorium, it was evident that the production would be a novel one. The setting was in full view under white, baleful illumination not unlike a work light. Large, plain, off-white walls (slightly textured) angled across the extreme sides of the stage; an unadorned drop of similar color hung at the rear. The white floor completed the effect of a vast cubic emptiness, an arid, shelterless world. Overhead, there hung a large rectangle of corroded copper or perhaps rusted iron. There was an old wooden bench or two . . . and actors starting the dialogue before the house lights had begun to dim.

No music, no fanfare, no warning; is it a mistake? Kent, Gloucester, and Edmund talking before the auditorium is dark, their voices remarkably quiet—forcing the audience into a surprised and abrupt stillness. The leather costumes are as starkly simple as the set: black, brown, deep olive, and liver-colored, all heavy and showing the patina of great wear and age, like the metal sheet above. Obviously the particulars of time and place are of no interest here; the feeling evoked is of something both ancient and ageless.

The throne, too, is environed in decay; it is backed by a large rusted slab, an object as weatherworn as the king who sits in front of it. This is no Grand Monarch, nor prehistoric chieftain, neither. Short, straggly beard, unkempt hair, basically the same kind of costume as the others. He is lean and eroded, part driftwood, part old man, all growl and gristle. The voice, in fact, is the biggest shock of all. As he divides his kingdom, the old man drones out his questions and commands in a drawling rasp chopped with the unexpected hitches and eccentric stresses of someone very old, bored, and edgy. The droning, tolling voice lulls one into half-attention and then the oddly stressed syllable, the curious pause catches by surprise. The body, too, interrupts its basic weariness with not quite spastic rhythms. And the characterization is not the least concerned with big effects or with time. The gait is slow, the speech is slow, and in this relentless slowness we see a man: mean, willful, irascible. This Lear of Scofield's is far less than heroic, quite a bit more than picturesque. Wary, plain, cold, worn, hard—like the set.

In fact, the whole production is in accord with the calculated monotony, the dry, astringent simplicity already noted. Pathos seems to be deliberately avoided. Long silences abound. Tableaux-like effects transfix particular moments as unexpectedly as Scofield's readings quietly magnify forgotten lines.

Two hours later the first half of the play is ending, and the house lights again illuminate both audience and action. The just-blinded Gloucester stumbles out, unaided, past indifferent, hustling servants clearing the stage, as we are

o

(Opposite) **Peter Brook's *King Lear:* The Court.**

caught unsheltered by the sudden glare of light. The strange way in which the play began was clearly no accident.

Certain scenes stand out sharply. At Goneril's house, this Lear's followers are interpreted so as to make Goneril's charges against them seem just. As one reviewer will write, "it is a little as if a senile Marlon Brando had come with a hundred wild ones. When she puts them out, his long gaze at her is flint-hard while, with one deliberate gesture, he overturns the great oval table . . . and signals his gang to wreck the place."[31] Furniture and cups fly about in a vicious orgy of destruction, which seems all the more violent in a production where movement has been kept as sparingly deliberate as in a game of chess.

The famous storm scene, which so often fails in production, is handled in a manner most memorable. It begins with two more heavy metal shapes looming ominously down into view; moved by an unseen force, the three thunder sheets begin to vibrate, shuddering waves of sound darkly over the impassive brightness of the stage. Augmented with electronic music, the sound is restrained but intense, rich in intimations of things full of dread—distant armies, flood tides, low-throated wind tearing at the forests, deep grindings in the earth. Actors run, miming the wind, carrying their cloaks protectively in arcing billows over their heads. This is a storm which infuses rather than dominates the scene; somewhere fissures are appearing, quietly crumbling the walls of the cosmos—and Lear replies in the same voice, neither he nor the universe having need to shout.

Similar in conception, the battle scene is probably the single most characteristic and unforgettable directorial invention in this production, and the scene in which the desert emptiness of the set becomes the most threatening in feeling. Kneeling, tiny and alone in the center of this great, gaping, vacuous mortar of a set, the blinded Gloucester sits immobile, staring, waiting to be ground and crushed. Seemingly from all around us, the sound of the unseen battle swells to cover us and our mirror image, Gloucester. It is a terrifying, welling ocean of beating, rumbling: a vortex of dissonance, the mindless, monstrous tide of evil in nature overwhelming the speck of humanity on stage and the hundreds of us—alone—watching him.

With the feeling of infinite, merciless, indifferent nature—the production exists. This Lear does not so much die as get ground away by life—and after four hours the play ends as it began, graying off into the real life of the people watching it.

As might be expected, critical reaction covered a wide spectrum, from ecstatic raves to dismissals of the production as dull and boring. Kenneth Tynan, known for clear-headed and often laceratingly critical reviews, was so smitten by this *King Lear* that he altogether dropped his critical tools and wrote a rhapsodic appreciation of the event:

> **A great director . . . discovered . . . not the booming, righteously indignant titan of old, but an edgy, capricious old man, intensely difficult to live with. In short he has dared to direct *King Lear* from a standpoint of moral neutrality. The results are revolutionary . . . incomparable.**[32]

The same neutrality that sparked Tynan's enthusiasm drew a grave objection from *Time's* reviewer: "The fatal flaw that mars Paul Scofield's *Lear* is detachment. . . . Brook's intelligence has shaped a *Lear* that knows its own mind and sticks uncompromisingly to it. Unfortunately, there is a hole in its heart."[33] Several other critics found the production "cerebral," "more intellectual than moving," "a strain to listen to," and "wearisome."

Critical reaction varied, too, according to nationality. In England, the reaction to Brook's work was generally favorable. In Paris, as has been noted, the production won prizes, but in America the response was one of respectful disappointment. This reaction cannot, by the way, be written off as due entirely to the disgraceful acoustics which the company suffered through at the New York State Theatre in Lincoln Center. In Boston, where there was no special acoustical problem, the general reaction was much the same as in New York.

A rather interesting pattern emerges when a large number of the reviews from England and America are examined: Except for those which were completely enthusiastic or totally negative, the reviews tend toward a single structural design—they begin with great praise, calling the production important, significant, etc., but very soon begin to point out flaws, and often end their comments with an expression of dissatisfaction: "*Yes!*—but—well, not really" sums up the pattern.

From the published production log of Charles Marowitz, Brook's assistant director, we get a clear picture of Brook's concept of the play:

> **Our frame of reference was always Beckettian. The world of this *Lear,* like Beckett's world, is in a constant state of decomposition. The set . . . ginger with rust and corrosion. The costumes . . . textured to suggest long and hard wear. . . . There is nothing but space—giant white flats opening on a blank cyclorama.**[34]

Some of the specifics of the production seem to have been taken from Brechtian staging and more from Absurdism, but most importantly, inspiration was drawn from Polish critic Jan Kott's book, *Shakespeare Our Contemporary*. In this book Kott states *King Lear's* theme as "the decay and fall of the world," and the title of his chapter on this play gives Brook's production its metaphor: *"King Lear* or *Endgame."*

Many reviews recognized the metaphor, some mentioning Antonin Artaud, Beckett, and even Kott. That the production concept evoked vivid and appropriate responses is easily seen in the kind of images used by the critics to communicate how the play felt:

Peter Brook's *King Lear:* Goneril's Palace.

35

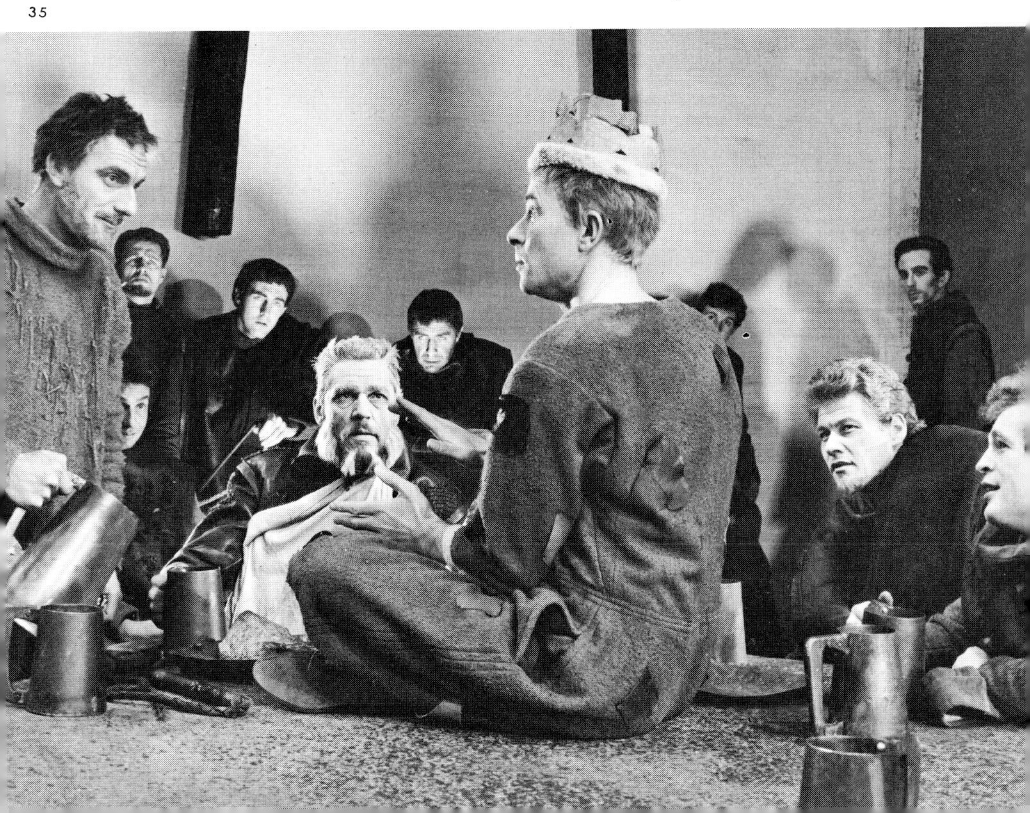

Of Lear himself:

He looks like the wood carving of a hard, peasant forester.[36]
looking like some rugged shepherd[37]
his bronze-crusted surface is impenetrable[38]
this Lear is an ikon—a mask with a monotonous eye[39]
carved from grey marble[40]

And of the characters in general:

like dolmens—ancient, broken, irregular stones[41]

Of the whole play:

A vengeful universe.[42]
Naked . . . magisterial simplification[43]
hangs suspended with a perfect quiet stillness[44] *the utterly still center of the hurricane, of the vacant eye.*[45]
We are . . . in everybody's old age where the juices have ceased to flow. Things grate. We grind our way further and further into deep holes of suffering, and the sound of our scraping fingernails is answered by thunder from an otherwise empty heaven.[46]

The majority of critics were deeply impressed with the quality of the performance, but this does not settle completely the issue of whether the production concept was well executed. As was noted earlier, a common review pattern began with great admiration and ended with reservations, sometimes very strong ones. One of the important objections concerned the pace of the acting. For many people four hours seemed quite long, and complaints about dismal, dreary, wearisome periods, particularly in the second half of the evening, were frequent. One can argue that the only way to create the feeling of a relentless, grinding, indifferent world is to play in a slow, abrasive manner—with really empty pauses. But the question arises: Is slowing down to the point of losing the audience's attention a valid approach, even in the execution of a nihilistic image? Could the world-view of *Endgame* and *Waiting for Godot* have been established in *Lear* without taking so much time? Probably. It is certain that Brook meant to communicate, and a performance tempo which tends to interfere with that communication cannot be called flawless execution of the idea.

But even if we assume that the tempo of this performance could have been stepped up to a point where the Beckettian slow decay was communicated without dimming the audience's attention, an important question still remains: Is the tempo and rhythm of Brook's image an accurate interpretation of Shakespeare's image?

The playwright, like the composer, creates an image which has a musical form—what Charles Marowitz refers to when he speaks of Brook describing to the cast "an overall theory of continuity and structure," the play's "innate rhythm." This important aspect of the play's meaning is probably the most difficult for the performers to grasp.

Rhythmic structure has to do largely with the order and tempo of action upon action (not the beat of stressed and unstressed syllables) and so—since some events necessarily take longer than others—rhythmic structure is intimately bound up in literal content. Thus, a certain overall tempo is implied in the text, and when an audience is bored and restless, it may be that the tempo of performance is too slow for the content being offered.

We know from Marowitz's notes that Peter Brook was especially concerned with rhythmic and playing-time problems at the first run-through, and was working on these problems in terms of his idea of the continuity and structure of *Lear* from then on. Therefore, we must take the performance tempo as a deliberate choice, not a "letting down" by the actors.

This book has already offered the analogy of a fugue to clarify the progressive momentum and complexity of *King Lear.* The image of an avalanche, crushing all life before it, also seems aptly to express the awesome effect of natural catastrophe and the terrifying acceleration of the play's movement. Brook's production enacted *Lear* not as an avalanche, but with the inch-by-inch grinding movement of a glacier; not as acceleration, but as slowing down—an apparent reversal of Shakespeare's pattern.

So questions of tempo and rhythm bring us to the final question: Is *Lear* really like *Endgame?* Kott, of course, thinks so, and his reasoning may be summarized as follows: he believes that the new theatre of our time can deal with the sort of "philosophical cruelty" he maintains was a contemporary reality to the Elizabethans, and that such a reality could not be dealt with in the environmentally conceived productions of the romantic and naturalistic theatres. Any realistic approach to the plot of *Lear,* Kott insists, encounters great difficulties; for if one looks for "psychological verisimilitude," one finds the exposition of Lear preposterous. It shows us a powerful king dividing his kingdom on the basis of a rhetorical competition among his daughters, and completely blind to the obvious hypocrisy of two of them. Gloucester, seen realistically, is no more convincing; both men seem naïve, stupid, and ridiculous. Their sufferings might arouse compassion, but not pity and terror. On the other hand, the Polish critic feels that a fairy-tale or legendary treatment of the exposition makes the cruelty of Shakespeare's world appear equally unreal. He thinks that the new theatre can both cope with the absurdity of the exposition and present the cruelty of the world, for in the new theatre "the tragic element has been superseded by grotesque"—which Kott finds to be crueler than tragedy. He finds the grotesque a dominant element in *Lear,* and his study emphasizes analogies between Shakespeare's play and those of Durrenmatt, Ionesco, and especially Samuel Beckett. He points up Shakespeare's use of clowning and pantomime devices: for example, the elaborate charade in which Edgar pretends to lead his blind father to the edge of a cliff is compared to Ionesco's use of an empty stage for the utopian Radiant City toured by the hero of *The Killer.* Gloucester's suicide leap is a tragic action, but the pantomime performed on the flat, empty stage is, a grotesque circus-like act, a "philosophical buffoonery" which Kott likens to Beckett's *Act without Words.*

Among Kott's most interesting observations are those on clowning and buffoonery as both "a philosophy and a profession" and on what he calls "the clown's play" that takes place at the center of *Lear,* in which a king and a blinded nobleman are srtipped to their naked humanity, and the king finally sees himself as the ridiculous creature the Fool has always seen. Kott sees the action of *Lear* as if played on two stages: the melodrama of the dividing of kingdoms, the acts of violence, lust, and betrayal, take place on what he calls "Macbeth's stage" and Kott regards these sequences as merely example and illustration, as a black realistic counterpart to what he calls the main scene: the action that takes place on "Job's stage." On this stage the "ironic clownish morality play on human fate" is enacted by beings who, like Job, are brought down and degraded and confronted with the cruel reality of their place in the universe. But whereas Job, even as a ruin of a man, talked to God and ultimately justified and ennobled his sufferings as part of an absolute order, such is not the case in *Lear*. While *The Book of Job* is to Kott a "theatre of priests," he finds that in *Lear* as in *Endgame,* it is as if *"The Book of Job* is performed by clowns," and the gods, cold and silent, do not intervene.

Peter Brook seems to have used only part of Kott's analysis—one had no sense in his production of events happening on "Macbeth's stage"—everything seems to have taken place only on "Job's stage."

Is Brook's image the one in the play? No critic has suggested that Brook's use of this idea was a gimmick; his production was sensitive and consistent to a degree that comes only from sincerity. Several writers who liked the interpretation, especially the wildly enthusiastic ones, seem by their approval to endorse the proposition that *Lear* is an Absurdist play. And whatever else may be said about it, this interpretation was not only astonishing and in part awe-inspiring, it convinced some of the best critics in several countries that Brook had uncovered elements which are actually in the play, but which no one had ever brought to the stage before.

On the other hand, the American director and critic, Harold Clurman, represented numerous voices when he felt that not enough of Shakespeare's world found its way into this "wasteland" treatment:

> **The world of Shakespeare's *Lear* is so rich in substance that one would be glad to dwell in it; we are rewarded for**

> **its agony by the fullness of its matter. Such a world may be full of horror: it is not *absurd*. . . . Shakespeare's world, however deprived of "solace," is one worth living in; Beckett's is not worth a damn.**[47]

Were the interpreters of this *King Lear* conscious of this problem? Again, the production log indicates they were, and that what cuts were made in the script of this production were made to remove any "reassurance" or "tint of sympathy." Any trace of tragic catharsis was to be avoided, and everything was done to create a vision of the world much more barren than Shakespeare's own.

What the more enthusiastic partisans hailed in this production was the recruitment of Shakespeare into the ranks of the Absurdists, but is he really any more Absurdist than he was Romantic when that earlier avant-garde made him their hero in the nineteenth century? Is Shakespeare as morally neutral in *King Lear* as Brook's production has made him seem? Does Shakespeare recognize no guilty parties, are there no innocent and/or heroic people held up for our admiration? The very fact that repentances, sympathies, and affirmative acts had to be pruned out by Brook is proof enough that as the playwright conceived it, *King Lear* is not *Endgame*. In fact, Brook's cuts deliberately censored Shakespeare's intentions.

Is this widely hailed production to be considered a failure, then? Should it never have been done? Such a position would be ridiculous on the face of it. No production can be dismissed which has led performers of the stature of Laurence Olivier to confess that, whether they liked it or not, they could not do *Lear* again without taking this interpretation into account. This was a production seriously undertaken, carefully carried out by some of the most talented people in the theatre; it was not a whimsical experiment, but a sincere effort to communicate certain insights, which it communicated with considerable success. For these insights we are forever in the debt of this company. However, as Robert Brustein put it, "one comes away from this performance aroused but unsatisfied, having witnessed not the definitive production of the play but rather a fascinating essay on it by a brilliant modern commentator.[48]

PART FIVE: **Some Final Issues**

It is true that craftsmanship in the arts is often simply a matter of skill, mere expertness devoid of concept, empty of creativity. It is equally true that those who shun arty notions like aesthetic theories and place their faith in artistic proficiency have nevertheless based their choice on a theory: an idea that artistic meaning is too nebulous to bother with, that one need only develop a superb degree of skill and all else will be added unto him. Craftsmanship does, therefore, depend on an idea of what art is and how it works.

As presented here, the idea of what theatrical art is includes the key proposition that artistic import is not so mysterious after all. For some this will seem bad news. For others it will be understood as opening the door a bit wider to greater creativity.

Historically speaking, to ask how anything may be said to have meaning is, of course, a new question, a startling and revolutionary one. And it was only a matter of time until this kind of concern with meaning led to the question of how a play means—this, too, being a question which nobody had ever really posed before. In terms of useful and constructive as distinct from purely theoretical ideas, this was perhaps the most important breakthrough in understanding the nature of drama since Aristotle's essay. As this book has tried to show, the question turned out to be eminently answerable, and the answers quite valuable.

For if the mysterious part of dramatic meaning is metaphor, then why not use metaphor—ideas of feeling—to analyze it? Is there any concrete evidence that theatrical form is fundamentally a matter of images; do competent theatre artists, though innocent of this theory, ever use associational or metaphoric techniques to understand a play, to invent artistic ideas? Even cursory checking shows that they do, constantly. Does this metaphoric thinking help toward more effective interpretation, toward more vigorous invention? As it has been said, genius is neither a trade nor a profession, and no method can of itself insure high creative achievement. But there are craft methods which make sense according to the particular problem at hand, and if it is the nature of drama to embody meaning in forms which work figuratively rather than literally, then it makes sense to shape our ways of working accordingly. So it happens in this book that a combination of theory and observation of practice has brought us to an idea of what theatrical art is—an idea which shows how creativity can be given its maximum effectiveness. It is in this sense that the door has been pushed open a bit more, and that would seem to be a very worthwhile thing.

But for some, the news is annoying. It puts us under new obligations. Knowing that drama operates by metaphor obliges us to train ourselves in associational as well as literal thinking. And seeing this, we cannot escape the further implication that has been so heavily stressed here: if the whole meaning of a play can be determined much more closely than we have been accustomed to believe, then so can the playmaker's intentions. Gone is the comfort of mystery. In floods the possibility of new and tougher critical standards. Of course, one can and should welcome the raising of critical standards as a healthy thing; it is likely to improve the general quality of the art it gauges. And if there ever was an era in which rampant eclecticism, bewildering diversity of artistic purposes, and strenuous insistence on The New threatens to annihilate our ability to evaluate art—our own creations or anybody else's—we are in it now. So the possibility of more accurate interpretations, better production concepts, and more demanding criticism would also seem to be a good thing.

Is it so bad, then, to ask, "Is there no right way to interpret a play?" Since this question was used at the outset as a springboard into the main discussion, it seems fitting to end the book with a final consideration of criticism and the issues which this seemingly impertinent question raises.

"Is there no right way?" is an interesting query in a way which has had no previous attention in this book. It is interesting because this question, or ones like it, usually produce such heated reactions. No matter which extreme one inclines toward—an Absolute Infinity of Interpretations, or the One-and-Only Answer—the result is the same. Annoyance and outright indignation are provoked by sharp inquiries into the validity of any interpretation. It is always as if someone had committed a felony.

Have we not risen safely above the bad old days when ethics went hand in hand with value judgments in the arts? On the surface it would seem so. And heaven knows, no one wants to return to Grandpa's naïve confusions of the Good, the True, and the Beautiful. Yet, to suggest that some enjoyable and highly original interpretation of a great play might be wrong is to ask for flared nostrils, heavy breathing, and loud voices. Can it be that though we no longer believe in mixing ethics with aesthetics, we still get morally indignant over brainless distortions of great plays—still become morally incensed over ungrateful attacks on brilliant interpretations?

It is a little embarrassing, in this Beckettian age, to have moral questions raised in discussing art theory—but in the interpretative arts, however we try to avoid believing it, the question of right and wrong interpretations can be considered a moral issue. Those who accuse Reinhardt, Hopkins, Jones, Guthrie, or Brook of doing wrong productions of Shakespeare's plays, though they may speak in gentlemanly tones, are nevertheless accusing the interpreters of a crime against Shakespeare, and the defenders rise in anger born of a sense of injustice being done to the interpreters. The available defenses are two: either to protest (and attempt to prove) that this *is* what Shakespeare meant, or, failing that, to fall back to the position that since nobody can know what a play means, each interpreter is free from any responsibility except to do the play as he happens to see it. In other words, either there was no crime, or it was justifiable homicide.

If both sides of the argument do not accept the premise that a playwright's greatness cannot be divorced from his artistic intentions, that the audience must not only be entertained but has the right to see him accurately performed, and that therefore the performers have an obligation to both author and audience which can only be called moral—then there is no basis for serious critical discussion of any production except box office success.

This is not to say, of course, that there must be a new rule of law which will force all interpreters into selfless searching for accurate productions of great plays. Everyone should be free to show his genius in any way he likes. But it is to say that we should be honest about why we get exercised about these matters. Responsibilities *are* involved. And there are standards available for judging interpretative concepts if we wish to use them. The price of creative freedom is high, for when the interpreter "has used Shakespeare [or any other great playwright] to create his own work . . . we expect him to prove, by his production, that he had the right to do so."[1] And proving that right means, in effect, making a new play that is as important as Shakespeare's.

The issue is a sticky one, for it is precisely the brilliant and talented interpreters who are most apt to need deep-probing criticism of their work. The efforts of incompetents may be deplored and forgotten; it is when brilliant and convincing lies are being told that the critic, even at the risk of being called an ingrate and a spoilsport, is obliged to practice his craft most vigorously.

For when the critic becomes merely an appreciator, he assists in the destruction of standards, not only of criticism, but of theatre art as well. In America this is exactly what seems to have been happening, at least as far as newspaper criticism of the theatre is concerned.

The discussion of the Hopkins-Jones *Hamlet* began with a comment on the extraordinary quality of the critical writing, and an examination of the extended excerpts from various reviews included in the appendix offers a really striking contrast to the newspaper drama criticism of today, in which so few reviewers write with either memorable style or content. An examination of why the critical writing in the *Hamlet* debate was so good offers instructive insights into the requirements for good criticism.

One reason for the disparity between the criticism of of the twenties and today is obvious: no critic came to the performance of *Hamlet* as a merely passive appreciator of one more new experiment; and on the opposite side, no believers in Jones's interpretation hid behind the view that there is no right way to interpret a play and that it is impossible to argue about the meaning of art. All the participants fought the good fight: they had distinct points of view and they expressed them with deep, and therefore sometimes eloquent, conviction.

The striking fact is that everyone had vigorous ideas of what theatre ought to be in this lively period of American theatre. No one assumed that it was impossible to define dramatic art or argue about the effectiveness of an interpretation. It had not yet occurred to anyone that the critic must beware of stifling the artists' creative individuality by demanding that they make the meaning of their productions clear to the audience, nor that each novel innovation must be treated tenderly as the potential art of tomorrow because "genius makes its own rules." In short—unlike what seems to have happened today—none of these critics felt so strongly the need to be tolerant that they were scared out of their profession. They all seem to have realized that good dramatic criticism depends on the conviction that the answer to "Is there a right way to interpret a play?"—is yes.

> **Taste changes, fashion changes, and the face of beauty changes from age to age. But the laws that govern creation, whether of matter or of man or of art, do not change. To maintain that there are no fixed standards in the arts, no points of reference, no guiding lines, is to excuse the lazy, to comfort the confused, and to abdicate responsibility.**
>
> *Marya Mannes*[2]

Appendixes

APPENDIX A: **Plays on Film**

The devastating loss which causes mere description of a performance to be all but worthless beside the real thing is such a handicap that the obvious solution is to select at least some interpretations which can be replayed—performances on film. Wearily, one hears the instant objection that a book on theatrical art is no place for a treatment of movies. That there are fundamental differences between the two modes seems so easy to recognize that one hesitates to waste time mentioning it. And—despite the champions of "pure cinema"—the fact that drama and film are often alike in fundamental ways seems so inescapable that one is embarrassed to have to bring it up.

Of course, merely to take a movie of a staged play is to fail to translate one medium into the other. Is there anyone who still does not know this? On the other hand, plays produced directly for motion pictures and television can result in genuine works of art while not in the least failing to be dramatic. As directors and designers who have worked in both media can testify, though the required techniques may vary radically, many of the artistic problems are identical in principle. This is particularly true in the area of main concern, the interpretation of dramatic meaning. In fact, it is possible to speak of interpretative ideas which would apply equally well whether the production were being conceived for the camera or a live audience. And that is exactly what most of the comments have been limited to in the discussion which follows. Also, let it be said that since filmed play interpretations can be reexperienced complete and intact in every detail, this unique advantage overrides the contention that interpretations invented by film makers must never be considered by those who work for the stage.

Finally, it should be said that while these productions do allow us to see the complete performance as it was first presented, some change of the original meaning still occurs as a result of removal from the original context of time and audience.

For the obvious advantage of utilizing a widely shared fund of knowledge and interest, the examples have once again been limited to classics. For those with further interest in filmed plays, a few of the more interesting ones have been listed in Appendix B.

Max Reinhardt's **A Midsummer Night's Dream**

Produced by Warner Brothers, 1935; directed by Max Reinhardt (and William Dieterle)

This film is interesting not only as an original interpretation of a great play, but also as a sample of Reinhardt's work—the work of a man whose international reputation in the living theatre is legendary, and who vividly personified the modern view of the director as one who conceives and controls the entire production.

A Midsummer Night's Dream has a consistency of style missing from some more recent Shakespearean films, and the interpretation is firmly based on an image, an image Reinhardt had developed, tested, and revised in eleven separate stage productions between 1905 and 1930. In the film which resulted from this lifelong involvement with the play, visual effects pour over the screen in an ever-increasing richness. Supported by troops of fluttering fairies, the actors loll, march, chase, and tumble; not only does the production make use of full-blown ballet choreography, but the total graphic feeling is like a flow of bright palace crescendos, dusky forest cadenzas, pizzicato glimpses of glistening dewdrops, and largo passages of mysterious and lovely moonlit creatures—the whole thoroughly and ornately orchestrated for the eye. In other words, Reinhardt's metaphor appears to be essentially this: *A Midsummer Night's Dream* looks like Mendelssohn's music sounds. The Mendelssohn music is, in fact, used through most of the film, and is the prime form-giving element; thus—whether it was intended to or not—it becomes the "purpose" which gives this particular production its meaning.

It would be too easy and also quite wrong to perfunctorily condemn this production simply because it is an arty stylization based on a Victorian translation of the play into music. The fact is that for all its faults (and they are grievous ones) this film is enjoyable, sometimes delightful entertainment, and has had an influence too pervasive for it to be dismissed as just a silly interpretation. Twice since the film's release, the Old Vic has produced this comedy in a manner very like the Reinhardt work, and indeed it has become almost traditional to think of this play in terms of Mendelssohn's music, ballet interludes, and sets and costumes to match. Nor is Reinhardt the sole inventor of the tradition: from Beerbohm Tree to the present there has been a strong tendency to embellish the lush language of this play with staging at least as luxurious. It may not be

Shakespeare, but this Mendelssohn-accompanied Disneyland treatment is certainly impressive and fun. And what does one say, while the memory of the film lingers, to the challenging question: "Well, if you don't like it this way, how *else* would you film *A Midsummer Night's Dream?*" The Old Vic's stage versions provided no new answer, and the Hallmark Company's TV version of *The Tempest* indicated that this approach to Shakespearean fantasy is by no means a thing of the past.

Reinhardt's film, *A Midsummer Night's Dream:* A Faery Palace.

1

Assuming that there *must* be another way to handle such a film, one has to ask to what extent Reinhardt's interpretation is unsatisfactory. He asserted that he wanted the picture to be "Shakespeare and nothing but Shakespeare"; but was he—on the contrary—really trying to fit Shakespeare to Mendelssohn? That is the effect of the film. Not only do we have its admirably unified Mendelssohn design, we also know Reinhardt as a name synonymous with impeccably preplanned production concepts. This nineteenth-century approach to Shakespeare is a thoroughly calculated stylization, and one has only to experience its music-oriented performance to appreciate that it is the playwright who has been brought to the composer and not the other way around.

Is Mendelssohn's music an accurate translation of the play? Assuming for the moment that it may be, one is immediately reminded that this work is used as a standard example of "incidental" music which fails as such because it has too much genius of its own ever to be incidental. And Eric Wolfgang Korngold's arrangement of it for the film points the music up, not down. This discussion, moreover, takes the view that Mendelssohn's music feels more like German romanticism than Elizabethan comedy. The fabric of Shakespeare's play, though brilliantly romantic and richly patterned, is as light and thought-borne as the words of which it is woven; the plushly exciting music of Mendelssohn follows a more massive design—it has the kind of Victorian solidity about its romanticism that conjures up forest glades of Wagnerian grandeur in which real rabbits and fauns seem quite at home. The magic woodland creatures of Shakespeare's imagination seem to be of a kind which cannot be impersonated by live bunnies and midgets. Thus, one can conclude that the image in the production is not the one in the script.

Yet the result, as has been pointed out, is not ludicrous. The audience gets some of the best of both Shakespeare and Mendelssohn, for the two works are certainly not completely at odds with one another. Besides, the commanding image chosen for this performance is not only well executed, it is sufficiently in the neighborhood of the playwright's idea to require no drastic rewriting. The words and most of the plot are Shakespeare's and much of the dialogue is well read, for some of the unlikely Hollywood "names" turned in surprising performances. The performance of the Pyramus and Thisbe interlude is memorably hilarious. Joe E. Brown

2

Reinhardt's film,
A Midsummer Night's Dream:
Pyramus and Thisbe.

as Thisbe, Hugh Herbert as Wall, and James Cagney as the outrageously enthusiastic, but histrionically hopeless, Bottom the Weaver, brought to this scene an unabashed love of low comedy which makes it one of the high points of the production. (The image for this playlet was not Mendelssohn, but Hanswurst, Pickelherring, and Mack Sennett.) And most of the costumes are admirable, the settings and costumes being typical of the director's practice of finding an appropriate stylization.

But in this stylization by Reinhardt "appropriate" is not quite equivalent to "organic." The film suffers from distortion of both the script's original form and from rather extreme preciousness. The rhythmic development of the play's action is freely interrupted by Reinhardt in order to let the *corps de ballet* perform fairy dances to the music. The director interpolates other nondramatic but intriguing goings-on, some of which are really disturbing. For instance, the grotesquely disguised midgets who play for fairy concerts (and "speak" in incoherent grunts) are ugly and unwholesome rather than charming. Reinhardt's Oberon (played by Victor Jory) is a solemn, humorless, rather threatening figure, a gloomy bogeyman commanding armies of batmen out of a Dracula movie. Is the audience supposed to feel happy when the reunion of Oberon and Titania is celebrated by having his batmen capture her glittering follies-girl attendants? These distortions and additions are bad enough, but finally, it is overpowering sweetness that does the film in.

Its award-winning cinematography decorates the film with halo haze and forest shadow; battalions of flying things—sprites, batmen, choruses of tittering fairies dripping with sequins; magic mist and moonbeam ladders—all rushing, fluttering, drifting, flushing, glooming, glittering—and by the time it is over what is badly needed is the ordinary light of day, and a bromo.

The image communicates all right, with a vengeance in fact, but the richness of Mendelssohn ladled over the richness of Shakespeare and supercollosified in Hollywood whipped cream—is all somehow too much.

Although the film can still be worth sitting through for its entertainment and historical values, as an interpretation of the play it illustrates a carefully organized image that was definitely not a solution to the problem of communicating the author's intent to a particular kind of audience. The film's failure at the box office was probably due in part to this weakness, and could serve as an object lesson to present-day advocates of popularization through spectacle; for though one might think that mass-audience appeal could be obtained by such decorative emphasis, Reinhardt's *Dream* did not succeed in attracting the mass movie audience of its day.

Orson Welles's Macbeth

Produced and directed by Orson Welles, 1948

In any modern production of *Macbeth,* how to play the witches is a key translation problem. Though their actual appearances onstage are few and brief, the witches are supernatural presences whose influence on the entire story is crucial and must have been felt more keenly by Elizabethan audiences than is possible today. Some in Shakespeare's audiences probably scoffed at the very idea of sorcery, but it was a time in which King James himself not only believed in such things, but wrote a book on demonology in order to refute another author's upstart disbelief. It was, in short, an era when black magic, prophesy, and witchcraft could be taken quite seriously on stage. However, now that fear and worship of science has all but replaced the fear and worship of demons, it is very difficult to make the weird sisters in *Macbeth* seriously believable, and because of this, difficult to keep the audience aware of their importance to the plot. In 1921, Robert Edmond Jones, very much aware of this problem, surmounted his setting for the play with three gigantic witch masks from whose eyes spotlights shone down to reveal the action below. Though bold and imaginative, this resort to scenic diagraming of Shakespeare's idea did not work to Jones's satisfaction, and the experiment showed that visual design alone does not solve the problem. The desire to recapture the originally serious and exciting effect of the witches has led to any number of rather extreme solutions. One of the more interesting of these was Orson Welles's staging of *Macbeth* for the Federal Theatre's Harlem company in 1936.

Working with an all-Negro cast for Harlem audiences, Welles translated the play in terms of the West Indies, interpreting the witches as practitioners of voodoo. This translation of the witches seems to have been a particularly successful aspect of this production, bringing the intended seriousness of the evil-working magic much closer to the audience's experience than a straight "Elizabethan" presentation could have done.

No doubt recalling this effective device when planning

his much later film version of the play, Welles again decided upon a primitive voodoo-like characterization for his witches. Perhaps reasoning from this idea, he developed an overall concept in which the play was seen as a conflict between savage paganism and newly arrived Christianity. This was an arresting idea to bring to the play, and in its execution Welles achieved a number of striking and meaningful effects, as well as several which are considerably less fortunate.

Most interesting are his solutions to the problems of making the witches plausible and pointing up their influence. The film opens with hands working over a cauldron from which they extract a shapeless, slimy mass; this is quickly shaped into a man, and capped with a small inverted crown, the spikes of which gouge cruelly down into the soft mass. Clearly a kind of voodoo doll, this object established the evil and prophetic power of the witches in a manner both theatrically compelling and sufficiently familiar to American audiences, but one which successfully avoids associations with anything like Halloween broomstrick riders or the creatures of Charles Addams. The voodoo idea helps create an effect for the end of the film which, in the sheer excitement of its theatricality, seems pure genius. Macbeth finally turns to do battle with Macduff; their ferocious encounter erupts jaggedly into the light as they lunge and slash through dead black shadows; suddenly we are staring at Macduff, his sword cocked for a murderous, tree-felling swing—in a flash the voodoo doll fills the scene; its head pops off, rolls away—then we see the feet of the real Macbeth sway, and the dark bulk of his body topple heavily into the blackness.

3

Orson Welles's Film, *Macbeth:* A priest.

4

Orson Welles's film, *Macbeth:* Dunsinane.

Other aspects of the Christianity-versus-paganism concept produce striking moments, especially in the pictorial effects. Duncan's army bearing crosses—seemingly thousands of them filling the sky—is an effect reminiscent of the work of Sergei Eisenstein, and a memorable one. But, as was suggested earlier, not all the consequences of this production concept are so easy to praise, nor is the concept itself executed with anything like the consistency of the one Olivier adopted for his film *Hamlet.*

Inconsistencies in the execution of ideas account for many of the weaknesses of this production. Though Shakespeare does not seem to have felt the need, bringing on the witches periodically to remind audiences of their controlling influence makes sense in terms of what Welles was trying to do. By doing such things as holding a dagger before the eyes of their voodoo doll, the witches are shown creating even the hallucinations of Macbeth; however, the idea is not thoroughly carried out: when Lady Macbeth makes her famous plea for evil spirits to appear and strengthen her, there is no hint of witchcraft at work. If the point is that the powers of evil deliberately fail her, then nothing has been done to make this point—on the contrary, the constant coming and going of these "spirits" has led us to expect a clear action from them, especially at a moment like this.

An even more important inconsistency has to do with the communication of the contrast between the Christian and pagan elements. The difference in behavior and attitude between the good Christians and Macbeth, who has been snared by the powers of darkness, is never made clear enough to carry the point. Welles's concept apparently intends to emphasize Macbeth's capture and damnation at the hands of Satan's agents, yet he includes scenes in which the good and noble King Duncan is shown savagely punishing the traitor Cawdor—a scene which Shakespeare kept off the stage—and Banquo, written as a rather noble, honest lord, is shown wigged, costumed, and acted as if he were none other than Attila the Hun. In brief, the "good guys" are indistinguishable from the "bad guys" in either behavior or appearance, and so the desired image of pagan-Christian conflict is all but lost.

Another element or concept crops up to confuse the film because it turns out to have nothing to do either with the over-all religious idea or with the original script: scenes between Macbeth and Lady Macbeth are played as husband-wife encounters with stress on physical intimacy and on sexual passion. On the basis of one or two lines in the script, much emphasis is later laid on their barrenness and its effects on this passionate couple. This slanting may be the reason that Welles felt obliged to bring Macbeth into Lady Macbeth's sleepwalking scene for a passionate embrace which wakes her into the nightmare of reality and sends her screaming from the room. Aside from being an unseemly intrusion on the actress's one big solo scene, this staging confuses the meaning of her exit speech, changing a reference to the need for stealth on the night of the murder—"to bed, to bed; there's knocking at the gate"—to something quite different.

Confusing inconsistencies in the treatment of period and location represent still another flaw in the interpretative ideas upon which this production is built. Except for the use of muted plaids, the costumes uniformly suggest a barbarous era not very specific as to time and place. Nor is a definite time and location indicated by the often fascinatingly gloomy and savage settings. It is hard to understand, then, why the characters speak with a slight Scottish burr, as if the production intended to add geographical and historical authenticity to what is otherwise poetic evocation of a brutish and ancient land. Judging from early reviews, the film presently available is a revision of the original, in which the burr was so heavy as to be almost unintelligible at times. Of course, Shakespeare could and did write in dialects when the dialect made some dramatic point, but since all the characters in *Macbeth* are Scots, no essential point is made by the use of the Scottish accents. The scenery seems to have been designed metaphorically rather than in terms of historical accuracy, and as a whole this approach seems preferable to the kind employed by the 1960 Hallmark television production of *Macbeth,* which spent a million dollars touring around Scotland to film the play in "accurate" costumes and castles, used a cast of 300, and for all this produced a rather musty, Beerbohm Tree effect without real excitement. It is a measure of his talent that Orson Welles's mistakes are more interesting as theatre than the careful and unoriginal productions of better financed but more conservative producers. Welles's scenic designer seems to have based his concept on Gordon Craig's vision of the play—"I see a rock surrounded by mist . . . in time the mist will wear away the rock"—and the vision is well captured in scenery composed of dripping caverns and walls. But these sets do not always work, for some are ambiguously designed and photographed so that locations become unclear. Are we on the blasted heath or on the wall of the castle? Is this a castle or is it a cavern? Are the witches floating on the mist or is that the floor of the studio? In quite a few shots, the economy in carpentry and the haste in setting up for shooting on a small production budget is too obvious, and the results confusing.

The production concept—or rather concepts—produced a number of additions and rearrangements, and it is hard to tell where sensitive and appropriate work on the script leaves off and inspired but arbitrary changes begin, because there are so many of the latter. Was it really necessary, for example, to write in a special scene of Duncan's army at prayer? And was it necessary that we hear the words of the prayer, written in a style so out of key with Shakespeare's? Another addition to bolster the main concept is the creation of a new character—the missionary monk, whose role was pasted together with lines chopped out of other characters' speeches. Other rearrangements abound; whole scenes in this production are actually patchworks of lines and speeches selected from various parts of the original and brought together into new combinations—as if Shakespeare were merely a man who created words and phrases to be redeployed by someone who really knows the theatre. This is all the more surprising since *Macbeth* (despite its commonly cited flaws) is one of the shortest and most tightly constructed of Shakespeare's tragedies. The result of the tinkering, as might be expected, is that many of the effects of the original are destroyed. In one odd example, Welles puts the scene of Macbeth's conversation with the doctor *before* rather than after the sleepwalking scene; having had its contents "anticipated" by what was once a recapitulation, the scene turns into an anticlimax.

Is the main image used for this production the one in the play? Shakespeare does seem to have intended the witches as minions of the devil whose "supernatural soliciting" sets in motion the basic events of the play; thus, an effective delineation of the script's religious values might well reinforce the main action—but that happens in the film only by fits and starts. Instead we get an incomplete statement of this main idea, a few other notions mixed in, and an ultimately confusing shuffling of the lines. The richness and originality of Orson Welles's great theatrical imagination is strongly evident in this production, but if skilled translation of the playwright's intent is to be our gauge, then this *Macbeth* is only an interesting experiment that misfired.

In fairness to the director, it must be added that this film production was risked under unusual circumstances. For its centennial celebration in 1947, the state of Utah commissioned Welles to produce and direct *Macbeth* at its state university. With typical ingenuity Welles conceived and directed the stage production so that it could be filmed with almost no changes. Having the enormous advantage of a totally preplanned "shooting script" for which all the actors knew their lines at the outset, the director was able to make *Macbeth* with what is probably an all-time film record in the efficient use of time and money. Unconcerned about the hazards of producing Shakespeare films, and uninterested in the originality of his feat, many reviewers poured scorn on Welles for the very fact that the film "was shot in less time than a cheap western." Admittedly, the special circumstances of the production account for some of its weaknesses, but this analysis, by concentrating on interpretative *ideas,* has tried to give an evaluation which is more objective and more accurate than those elicited when the film was first released.

Olivier's Hamlet

Produced by J. Arthur Rank, 1948;
directed by Laurence Olivier

> **My whole aim and purpose has been to make a film of *Hamlet* as Shakespeare himself, were he living now, might make it. It is easy to retort, "But Shakespeare is not living now, therefore you should not do this." Every Shakespeare film must, by its very nature, be a re-creation of a Shakespearean play in a quite different art-medium than that for which it was primarily intended. . . . If I did not consider the translation of *Hamlet* to the film to be a legitimate experiment, I would never have attempted it. You may be assured of that.**
>
> *Laurence Olivier*[5]

The film translation which Olivier directed did, of course, stir up inevitable controversy, for we have reached a state in which every third person in the world has had to memorize lines from the play, and will tell you how the production *should* have been done. However, before delving into the controversial aspects of the film, it is well to notice that of all the Shakespearean pictures that have been made to date, *Henry V* and *Hamlet*—both directed by Olivier—stand head and shoulders above the rest and have given millions of people not only their first viewing of professionally performed Shakespeare, but of Shakespeare greatly acted.

The film begins with a voice saying, "This is the story of a man who could not make up his mind." As if to prove this assertion, the voice then recites the famous "tragic flaw" passage from Act I, scene 4: "So, oft it chances in particular men. . . ." At least scores, possibly even hundreds of reviewers and critics delightedly seized on this and, while admiring the film's magnificent acting, dismissed the overall interpretation as silly because of the opening pronouncement on the sound track. In one instance an entire book was touched off by the way the film begins.[6] Unfortunately, the opportunity to criticize an important production of *Hamlet* apparently rattled these commentators, for they failed to notice that what actually happens in this film treatment seems to have nothing to do with the "interpretative" declaration with which it begins. Quite the contrary, Hamlet keeps making up his mind with precipitous abandon, and the typically virile playing of Olivier ignores the old romantic conception of the Prince as a kind of overly cerebral young Werther. Whatever the main interpertation, it had nothing very important to do with the film's rather curious preface.

As the voice tells us what the story is supposed to be about, a far more important comment is being made by the camera: we see a dark, mist-shrouded castle with a shaftlike tower, place and time indefinite; presently we are floating through its inner depths . . . up and up a twisting stairway to pause finally and steal a lingering glance at the first important object of life we have discovered in the castle—a grand and rumpled bed; we move on, as if in the plunging motion of a dream, and reach the heights of the castle where the dialogue begins. To these suggestive beginnings more obvious points are added: Hamlet's mother is still a very desirable woman, and they kiss squarely on the mouth, long and passionately. The men wear not only medieval-style hose, but codpieces, some fringed, and the camera at least once emphasizes this. Is this, then to be a Freudian interpretation of the play? Will the misty, ingrown sub-world of this shadowed castle represent the subconscious mind? Perhaps even the mind of Hamlet himself?

These questions do not go long unanswered. The sometimes strange swimming of the camera—though it tends to make the audience seasick—suggests a world of free association in which logically motivated movement does not apply. In fact, we descend quite literally into Hamlet's head and see with his eyes as he delivers the "To be or not to be" soliloquy. The speech is read from the top of the shaftlike tower, and in a final figure of impotence, his dagger slips from his hand and plummets far below into the sea. Hamlet's delay in avenging his father's murder stems from subconscious jealousy of his father, from his guilt feelings about his repressed desire to murder his father and have his mother for himself. So, according to Ernest Jones in *Hamlet and Oedipus,* and so too, apparently, in this film. At least, a strongly Freudian production concept is evident from the symbols and the action itself. Further checking confirms this: Olivier reverses the order of the "To be or not to be" speech and the "Get thee to a nunnery" scene, making the rift with Ophelia precede his dash to the tower, thereby implying that (in addition to his troubled feeling for his mother) his frustrated love for Ophelia touches off his desire to commit suicide.

Does the production suffer from preciousness? It is possible to find things to quibble about under this category —like burying the camera lens in the hairs of Hamlet's head—but in general the picture does not get distracted by its own performance ideas. Nor does it fall into demonstration or illustration. Perhaps it can be said that the Freudian symbols used are illustration rather than dramatic action, but the main point is made without relying on signs and devices which have to be consciously recognized. The kiss, the codpieces, the glimpse of Ophelia's leg, the generous bed on which Hamlet and his buxom mother wrestle—such things create a sensual atmosphere and the audience can be entirely innocent of Freud and still feel the steady accumulation of these devices. What has bothered many people is the way the proportions of the script have been altered to suit this translation.

Shakespeare would surely not have thought our present-day reader's version, which takes four and a half hours to play, a suitable length for performance, and it goes without saying that cuts have to be made. Also, transferring the action to the screen requires further changes, and nobody sensible to these necessities will carp at the mere fact of these changes. What is disturbing is the rearrangement—mentioned a moment ago—of certain sequences like the "Nunnery" and "To be or not to be" scenes. Again, while some would question on principle this kind of alteration, the real test is what it accomplishes, and in this instance it does change the sense of the script by creating a new inciting incident for the most famous speech in the play—a motivation for his speech which is not implied in the sequence Shakespeare himself selected. Such changes have little to do with the solution of cinematic problems, and would probably have been made in a stage production following the same ideas. This is also true of the valuable seconds taken to establish Freudian atmosphere through means not available in the dialogue. Since this latter purpose is much more efficiently served by the camera, it is not surprising to see that a really great amount of time is spent in camera work, and that some important passages have been cut along with the trivial ones in order to allow time for a kind of cinematic voyeurism: following Hamlet through tortuous corridors, stealing a look at the bed, seeing Hamlet ascend to the glistening tower, and so on. While this is criticism of the filmic aspect of Olivier's work, it is important to see that this use of the camera derives from the production concept and not from any strong desire to remake the play in purely cinematic terms.

Among the more important material cut was all that relating to Fortinbras, whose function in the original is interesting. The Elizabethans, politically conscious in gene-

Laurence Olivier's film, *Hamlet:* The Queen's chamber.

7

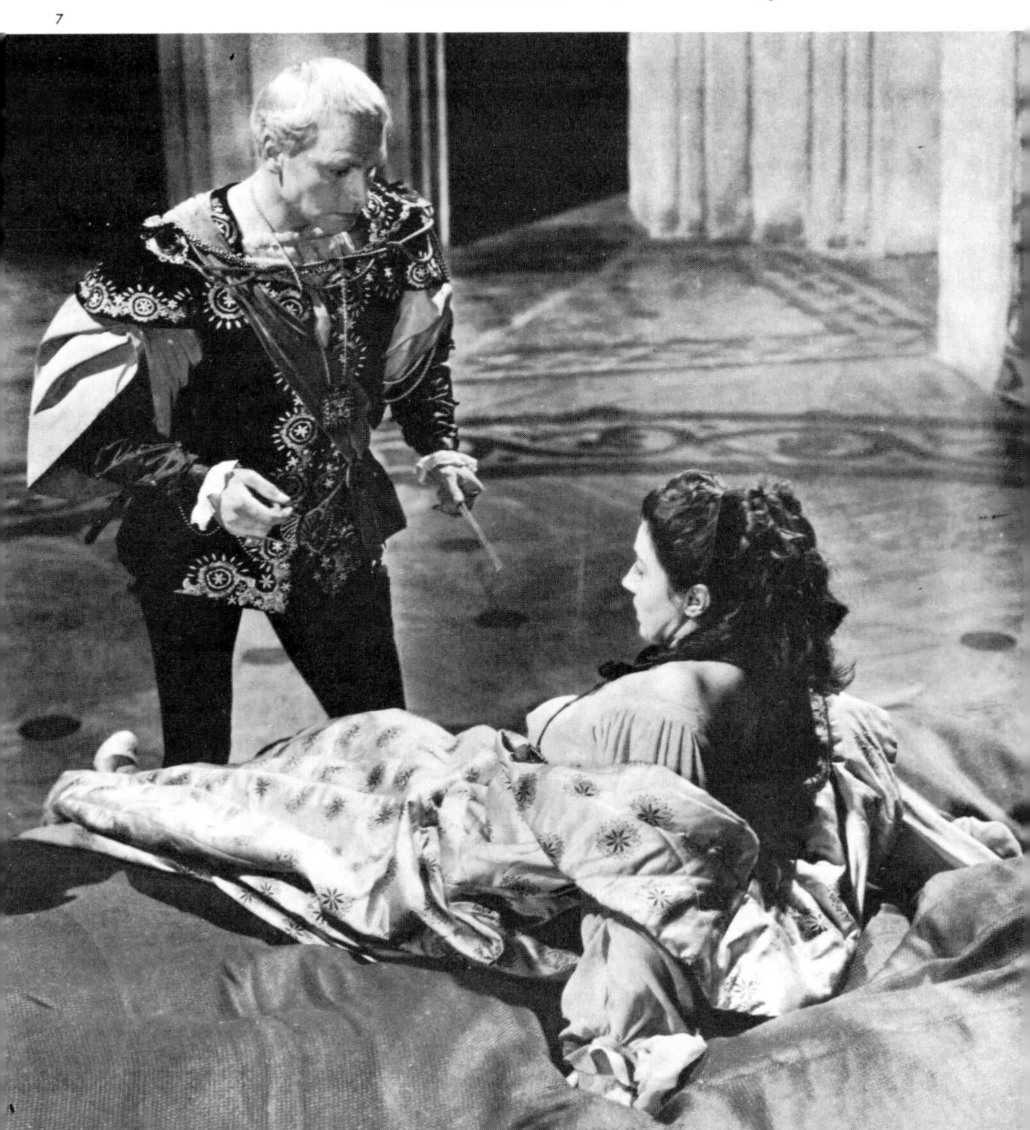

ral and particularly concerned about who would succeed Elizabeth to the throne, would have been disturbed to have seen a throne left empty at the end of the play; therefore Shakespeare supplies another prince, Fortinbras—whose very name means warriorlike strength—to stabilize the situation and insure future harmony. Though it can be argued that contemporary audiences care little, if at all, about Hamlet's successor, this does not mean that a modern translation requires the elimination of Fortinbras, for he still serves the very useful purpose of ending the play with satisfying finality.

Elizabethan drama was, by comparison with some of our own, quite extroverted and well in touch with the social passions of its time; from the first regular Elizabethan tragedy, *Gorboduc,* all the way to *King Lear* the intense interest in the political welfare of England manifests itself in the plays. *Hamlet* is no exception. While its focus is far more personal than otherwise, it is certainly not exclusively so. If Norway and Denmark were perhaps merely "other places" to Shakespeare's audience, Hamlet nevertheless lives in the real world. His is a kingdom with people in it, with citizens who are raised by Laertes when he intends to attack the king, and there are armies on the move, governments at stake—all this in the usual vein of Shakespeare's sense of social context. Not so in the film.

The Freudian image implies a clinically personal interest in this young man's problems, and this implication is followed with admirable consistency. The fact that he is a prince is not forgotten, but it becomes secondary. Fortinbras and his army disappear altogether; there is no sense of population in this misty kingdom, and the play becomes introverted—looking nowhere but down and into the mysterious, secret workings of a diseased court.

Is this sex image the soul of the play? If not, how

Laurence Olivier's film, *Hamlet:* Pursuing the Ghost.

important is it to the play's total meaning? Is it important enough to warrant an entire production devoted to it? As this evaluation of the production has shown, use of the Freudian image required such a strongly editorial approach as to cast very grave doubt on the strength of its kinship to the play Shakespeare wrote.

It may still be maintained that for today's psychologically oriented audiences this is a perfectly valid translation, but the fact remains that as a move away from the playwright's intent, it is not one imposed by the mere necessity of translation. Nor does the concept work with perfect ease and efficiency: as has been pointed out, it requires cutting which goes beyond the basic needs of film making and audience endurance; it means leaving out large pieces of what Shakespeare said in order to say the kind of thing that Ernest Jones has said. These changes in turn alter the rhythmic structure of the whole, and the elimination of Fortinbras leaves the play without a suitable finish—inadequately compensated for by a rather long, anticlimactic, crescendoing dirge during which Hamlet is slowly carried to the top of the castle. Thus, in spite of its often revealing, always interesting, and frequently powerful effects, this production concept does create some very troublesome distortion and cannot be regarded as a completely successful translation for modern audiences of Shakespeare's intent.

APPENDIX B:
An Annotated List of Twenty-two Filmed Plays

The catalogues of the rental agencies, listed at the end of this appendix, contain film versions of often-discussed plays, and the availability of these films makes it possible to assemble illustrative film anthologies on any number of special topics. One can have, for instance, a Shakespeare film series, a Shaw or an O'Neill series, or one on American drama from *Anna Christie* to *A Streetcar Named Desire.*

The following list is limited to productions having particular relevance to the subject of this book, and it represents only a tiny part of the vast number of films available for use in the study of drama and its performance. Shakespearean films are stressed, of course, though the list includes a few other works often studied in drama and literature classes.

Several of these plays have been filmed more than once, so that one can compare the relative merits of their different interpretations.

Three Versions of Macbeth

Macbeth, directed by Orson Welles (1948). The production discussed earlier in this book. Available through Brandon Films.

The Throne of Blood, directed by Akira Kurosawa (1958). A translation into melodrama by one of Japan's best film directors. Set in medieval Japan. Macbeth is interpreted as a power-hungry samurai. Available through Brandon Films.

Macbeth, directed by George Schaeffer (1961). Starring Maurice Evans and Judith Anderson. In color. First seen on the Hallmark TV program. Filmed on location in Scotland in an attempt to achieve a kind of "historical accuracy." Available through Audio Film Classics.

Three Versions of Romeo and Juliet

Romeo and Juliet, directed by George Cukor (1936). A lavishly mounted MGM "prestige" film, made in the heyday of the great studios, and starring Leslie Howard and Norma Shearer. Slow, old-fashioned, and romantic, it can nevertheless be viewed as what a competent nineteenth-century stock company production might have been like. The acting is generally pedestrian, but has a unity of style missing in more recent American efforts. John Barrymore's Mercutio is one of his best film performances. Available through Contemporary Films.

Romeo and Juliet, directed by Renato Castellani (1954). Starring Laurence Harvey and Susan Shentall, with Flora Robson. In color. Another attempt at doing a nonhistorical play on location in a historical setting, this version was filmed in and around Verona. Available from Contemporary Films.

The Ballet of Romeo and Juliet, directed by Lev Arnstam and Leonid Lavrovsky (1954). A Soviet color production starring Galina Ulanova and the Bolshoi Theatre Ballet Company, with music by Prokofiev. A ballet film which received critical praise, this version is useful in observing how much of the play can be communicated without dialogue, and, of course, basic differences between the dance and the drama. There is a running commentary in English. Available through Brandon Films.

Two Versions of Julius Caesar

Julius Caesar, directed by David Bradley, with Charlton Heston as Marc Antony (1950). Made on a shoestring by Bradley and some young collegiate and semiprofessional actors in the Chicago area (Heston was just another student at Northwestern at the time). A truly experimental and noncommercial venture, it is one of the few 16-mm films ever to receive commercial theatre runs, and it is in several ways more interesting than the later MGM version (below). Available through Brandon Films.

Julius Caesar, directed by Joseph Mankiewicz (1953). An "all-star" cast featuring John Gielgud, James Mason, Louis Calhern, and Marlon Brando as Marc Antony in his first appearance in a Shakespearean role. The attempt to render the streets of ancient Rome with picturesque realism—grubby and lived in—attracted favorable critical comment, though the domestic set-things are House and Garden Roman. Despite interesting elements, notably Edmund O'Brien's Casca, this film seems to have been overrated by the critics, perhaps because it was the first Shakespearean film out of the Hollywood studios since the 1930s. Available through Films Incorporated.

Single Productions: Shakespearean Plays

A Midsummer Night's Dream, directed by Max Reinhardt 1935). Film discussed earlier in this book. Available through Contemporary Films, Brandon Films, and Films Incorporated.

Hamlet, directed by Laurence Olivier (1948). Film discussed earlier in this book. Available through Contemporary Films.

Henry V, directed by Laurence Olivier (1945). In color. Olivier, Robert Newton, Leo Genn, and Felix Aylmer head a superlative cast. The most successful of all Shakespearean films, probably responsible for a revival of interest in filming Shakespeare. The choice of a theatrical stylization as opposed to a "pure-film" approach created some controversy when the film appeared. For statements of both sides of this issue, see Kenneth Macgowan's review in *Hollywood Quarterly,* October, 1946, and Daniel Krempel's "Olivier's *Henry V*: Design in Motion Picture," in the *Educational Theatre Journal,* December, 1950. James Agee's excellent and informative review for *Time* (April 8, 1946) is reprinted in *Agee on Film,* McDowell, Obelensky, 1958. Available through Contemporary Films.

Othello, directed by Orson Welles, with Welles, Michael MacLiammoir, and Suzanne Cloutier (1955). Filmed on Cyprus in a pictorially handsome style resembling Eisenstein's *Alexander Nevsky,* this film, even more than *Macbeth,* raises questions about how "filmic" a Shakespearean film can be before it begins to destroy the author's creation. Like most of Welles's work, it is at times infuriating, never dull. Available through Contemporary Films.

Richard III, directed by Laurence Olivier (1955). Lavish color film featuring almost every major Shakespearean actor in the English theatre at the time. Olivier's performance as Richard is striking, but the film is treated more as history than as the propaganda-melodrama it is; settings and costumes are in the historically accurate tradition, and the ending of the play is altered to conform with historical accounts of Richard's death. Available through Brandon Films.

Twelfth Night, directed by Yakov Fried (1956). A Soviet color film made on the shores of the Black Sea. Contains a hilarious performance of Aguecheek in the midst of a generally pedestrian production with an old-fashioned flavor. The actress playing Viola, by trick photography, plays her own brother, with occasionally disturbing results. Dialogue in English. Available from Brandon Films.

Other Films of Theatrical Interest

Antigone, directed by George Tzavellas (1962). A film version of Sophocles' tragedy starring Irene Pappas and Manos Katrakis, in Greek, with English subtitles. Well received by reviewers. Available through Audio Film Center.

Le Bourgeois Gentilhomme, directed by Jean Meyer (1960). A record of the Comédie Française production of the Molière comedy, in color. In French, with English subtitles. The production will seem mannered and overly reverent to some, but any production by "the House of Molière" is apt to be important to students of the theatre. Available through Contemporary Films.

Camille, directed by George Cukor for MGM (1937). Starring Greto Garbo, Robert Taylor, Lionel Barrymore. Garbo's performance makes the famous nineteenth century romantic play almost believable. Some fine acting in the supporting roles. Available through Films Incorporated.

Cyrano de Bergerac, directed by Michael Gordon (1950). Starring José Ferrer. A low-budget filming by producer Stanley Kramer of José Ferrer's Broadway revival of the Rostand play, made soon after its Broadway run. A good record of Ferrer's performance, though this is one time that a play suffers by not being made in technicolor on a budget of millions. Available through Contemporary Films, Brandon Films, Audio Film Center.

Le Mariage de Figaro, directed by Jean Meyer (1963). Record of the Comédie Française production of the Beaumarchais comedy, in color. In French, with English subtitles. Available through Contemporary Films.

Oedipus Rex, directed by Tyrone Guthrie (1957). The Stratford, Ontario, production discussed earlier in this volume. Available through Contemporary Films.

Tartuffe, directed by F. W. Murnau, with Emil Jannings 1925). A silent-film version of Molière's comedy, made by one of Germany's most famous directors of the silent era, and starring one of the period's most famous film actors. The film's visual style was much praised by Paul

Rotha in *The Film till Now* for capturing the spirit of the period of Louis XIV. Available through Brandon Films.

Volpone, directed by Maurice Tourner (1939). A French film classic of the thirties, this justly famous film of the Stefan Zweig–Jules Romains version of Ben Jonson's play stars Louis Jouvet and Harry Baur. A gallery of marvelous characterizations by leading French actors of the period in a richly mounted, acid production. Available through Contemporary Films.

Film Rental Agencies

Information about these films and many others available for study and film-festival showings can be found in the catalogues available on request from major rental agencies. Names and addresses of a few leading agencies are listed below:

Brandon Films, 200 West 57th Street, New York 19, N.Y.
Cinema Guild and Audio Film Center, 10 Fiske Place, Mount Vernon, N.Y.
Contemporary Films, 267 West 25th Street, New York 1, N.Y.
Films Incorporated, 1150 Wilmette Avenue, Wilmette, Ill.
Museum of Modern Art Film Library, 11 West 53rd Street, New York 19, N.Y.
Trans-World Films, 53 Jackson Boulevard, Chicago 4, Ill.
United World Films, 105 E. 106th Street, New York 29, N.Y.

A complete list of 16-mm film libraries is published by the Superintendent of Documents, Government Printing Office, Washington D. C. The cost is 70 cents.

APPENDIX C: A Note on Sources

The paragraph which follows represents the authors' idea of the book's most characteristic contributions—and the remaining four pages describe what has been accomplished elsewhere which enabled such a book to be conceived.

The following things appear to make this work different from other books which deal with some of the same problems:

1. Looked at from the long view of history, the semantic-inspired theory of artistic meaning is genuinely new, and this has been applied here to theatrical practice.

2. This application has made it possible to assemble various partial recognitions of the metaphoric principle into a single presentation, which reveals metaphorical thinking as the central principle of theatrical meaning and its interpretation.

The First Source: Theatrical Practice

There are two main sources for the general theory and the ways of working proposed in this book. The first source lies in the practices of the many theatre artists whose work has seemed stimulating and valid, and whose methods have shared such common attributes as to suggest the basis of a theory. The other source has to do with meaning theory and will be discussed in its turn.

Of all the artists of the theatre, it is Mordecai Gorelik who in advocating the use of scenic metaphor, has been the most articulate about the interpretative use of images. Although Gorelik has naturally talked in terms of scenery, he, more than any other person of the theatre, is to be given credit for breaking the ground for the kind of approach represented in this work. It is Gorelik's work as a practical man of the theatre, and his stimulating discussions of his working methods which really have been noticed by theatre people. A book like this would have come along sooner or later, but it is hard to imagine it coming sooner than it did without Gorelik's efforts.

Other scene designers have followed Gorelik's lead, and of these the authors are indebted to Lester Polakov for permission to observe his teaching at his Studio of Stage Design in New York City where his practices confirmed the practical value of the approach and helped to clarify some of the specific working methods described herein.

It should be pointed out that many of the practices from which the theory is derived, and even parts of the theory itself, are neither new nor revolutionary. The idea that a work of art is an organic whole antedates the theatrical practice of organic play production by many years. The sense of a need for "appropriateness" in theatrical production goes back at least to David Garrick (1717–1779) and was developed into a deliberate program of scenic and acting reform in the 1870s by the Duke of Saxe-Meiningen. Most of the practices in modern integrated production design were first articulated by Appia and Craig before the turn of the century and have since been elevated by their followers into the dominant mode of production in today's theatre.

The Second Source: Meaning Theory

The second main source—particularly for understanding the dynamics of dramatic meaning—is the current interest in the theory of meaning generally, and the new direction it has given to aesthetics. Although this movement has scarcely touched the writings of theatre people, it is at least thirty years old. Therefore, the place of theatre aesthetics in the development of this trend seems worth setting forth in the following summary.

Whereas the theories of Zola stressed scientific empiricism and assumed virtually absolute laws which determined man's behavior, recent aesthetic theorizing has assumed human mentality to be not passive as in the determinist view, but essentially creative, and has stressed relativistic relationships rather than absolute laws. In this change the move from Newton to Einstein is hard to miss.

The simple empiricism which had ushered in the age of science—reasoning by simple cause, the doctrine of a mechanistic universe—was swiftly modified by Einstein's hypotheses that time is not an absolute and that matter and energy are functions of another term (the speed of light). The Newtonian precepts, with their earthbound frame of reference, became "classical" and the new physics began to study a given problem in various "fields," levels, or contexts. In this manner, the interpretation of nature was cast in terms of *transformation,* not mechanical principles. And, as had been the case in the previous century, other sciences and disciplines anticipated, shared, or took up this new point of view.

Thus, anthropology has become increasingly interested in the transformation of values between cultures; psychology and sociology tend to merge where both become interested in the necessity of studying behavior in different contexts or "fields"; and books appear recommending the empirical method as only one of the four equally valid approaches to research.[1] *The Quarterly Journal of Speech* carries an article which asserts that the "[Newtonian] notion of cause, though sufficiently powerful to support classical mechanics, has now been rejected by systematic thought in many areas . . . its successor, whether so called or not, is transaction."[2] And so it goes.

Einstein's contention that "A correct proposition borrows its 'truth' from the truth-content of the system to which it belongs,"[3] and his similar statements about principles of significance, called into question the whole issue of how anything may be said to have meaning. That a new study of meaning should arise from such speculation is not surprising. Semantics and the still burgeoning interest in meaning have given aesthetics a new direction.

Thus far, in this new orientation of art theory a number of identical and similar concepts have been evolved independently by different people. A few statements will serve to show this:

> ***A philosopher on myth:*** **Thus the special symbolic forms [like art, myth, language] are not imitations but *organs* of reality, since it is solely by their agency that anything real becomes an object for intellectual apprehension. . . .**[4]

> ***A critic on art criticism:*** **In talking about things we have conceptions of them, not the things themselves; and it is the conception, not the things, that symbols [words] directly "mean." . . . The artistic insights we are considering appear rather as manifestations of this artistic imagination than as qualities which correspond with any external reality.**[5]

A painter on painting: The experience of an image is thus a creative act of integration. . . . Every force acts in a medium, exists in a field. Any process induced by forces makes sense only with reference to the surroundings, as an interaction between the force and the medium in which it acts.[6]

A psychologist on the visual arts: Art presents to one's eyes what he . . . believes to be true.[7]

These statements have been selected to show the kinship to relativism, to the idea of meaning as nonabsolute, which aesthetic thinking is beginning to pursue. However, the only *comprehensive* aesthetic theory along these lines is that of Susanne K. Langer. The groundwork of this theory is contained in her *Philosophy in a New Key,* pubished in 1942,[8] and the theory itself appeared in 1953 under the title *Feeling and Form.* Further clarification and discussion were forthcoming in *Problems of Art,* 1957.[9] Because of its systematic discussion of all the major arts and because of its chapters on the drama, *Feeling and Form* is of particular significance for those interested in the theory of theatre.

In the past quarter century the scores of books and hundreds of articles on language and meaning have touched on many fields of study: forensics, psychology, gesture, ethics, speech therapy, medicine, communication theory. Yet, only a small proportion of these publications deal specifically with art theory, and, of these, only a handful embrace aesthetics of the theatre. In sum then, the place of theatre aesthetics in the development of meaning analysis is both late and slight, though by no means insignificant.

APPENDIX D:
Extended Excerpts from the Newspaper Debate Over the Hopkins-Jones "Hamlet," 1922

The following portions of articles and letters, relating to the production of *Hamlet* discussed in Part Four, are included here to supplement that discussion. These examples also illustrate criticism which is symptomatic of a vital and living theatre—one than can provoke penetrating analysis and debate.

The New York Sun carried a generally laudatory review, headlined:

Barrymore Is Cheered When He Plays "Hamlet"
Arthur Hopkins Shares in the Tumultuous
Applause—Solid Interior Jones Setting
Provides Extraordinary Novelty

But the review was critical of several aspects of the production concept.

> Once more has Robert Edmond Jones, Arthur Hopkins's scenic artist, endeavored to improve on Shakespeare. He has provided a very beautiful solid setting, an interior in the castle with wide steps in the rear center leading up to a high arched, open doorway. . . . Such a setting created . . . a decided uncertainty in the minds of the spectators as to how certain scenes would be managed. One of Mr.

> Jones's devices, which brought to mind the "Follies" and Winter Garden revues, was to use a silk front drop and have the scenes played in front of it, thanks to an apron that had been built around the stage. Several scenes were managed by using other curtains that changed sufficiently the appearance of the stage. But the grave-digging scene proved an insurmountable difficulty and *Ophelia's* grave was dug inside of the castle, although the players and the audience acted as though it was a graveyard. Naturally, the illusion was spoiled. . . .
>
> Another innovation was an apparition and not an actor as the Ghost. . . . Reginald Pole . . . spoke the lines. You saw a long, moving figure of yellow light on a green screen. But it was more movie than moving, and the voice did not blend with the ghost. It was like having two ghosts, one that materialized and one that talked.
>
> But the solid setting was such an ideal background for beautiful stage pictures that its shortcomings are easily forgotten. Most beautiful of all was the moment before the final curtain, when *Hamlet's* body is carried silently by the soldiers up the stairway and out into the open air. It had the feeling of "A Grammarian's Funeral," Browning's majestic poem, and it seemed as though Hamlet was being borne along to be laid to rest on some mountain top.[1]

J. Ranken Towse, conservative critic of *The New York Evening Post,* wrote one of the most negative reviews, finding Barrymore's performance and the production as a whole "interesting, but without tragic power." He recognized what was new and good in this *Hamlet* while devoting much of his review to detailing Barrymore's shortcomings, but not until he had elaborated on the theme of his headline:

"Hamlet" Spectacle and Little Else
Latest Instance of a Great Play
Sacrificed to the Scenic Whims
of Modern Producers

Very seldom, if ever, has a great play even in the days of Irving or Beerbohm Tree, been presented with a more richly spectacular background. The stage pictures were notably designed and gorgeously brilliant or impressively sombre in color, while every grouping had been arranged with a view to pictorial effect. . . . Every precaution had been taken to secure an ideal representation except the important one of vital interpretation of the text.

The lamentable fact is that Mr. Arthur Hopkins, whose artistic instinct and ambitions need not be disputed . . . has fallen into very much the same error that made his "Macbeth" so sad a disappointment. He has not yet realized the fact that a costly and luxurious setting does not disguise, but rather emphasizes, the weakness of a poor performance. Moreover, he has become infected with some of the pernicious theories of Gordon Craig, and of what is called, by utter misnomer, the "new art of the theatre", which while comparatively innocuous in the case of modern exotic and abnormal drama, cannot be made to harmonize with the structure and spirit of those great classics in which the realistic and the imaginative are combined in incomparable fashion. To attempt to modernize Shakespeare, to apply to his robust and soaring genius the finicking methods of a more artificial civilization is not only futile but something worse than foolish. . . .

The foundation of [Jones's] spectacle is one majestic set, a vast domed chamber inclosing most of the stage, with platforms and steps leading up through a lofty arch to

> the open air beyond, and an eminence which served for the ramparts of the castle, and various things . . . but not invariably felicitous, while the front part of the stage he used as an apron, sometimes with curious effect, as in the prayer scene.
>
> As a matter of simple fact the scenic scheme . . . expressly devised to simplify and expedite the action, did nothing of the sort, but on the other hand, tended rather to delay and confuse it. . . . If the spectacular was served it was only too often at the cost of the destruction of all illusion. This was strikingly the case with regard to one of the most notable innovations of the whole spectacle: the abolition of the spectral Majesty of Denmark—"the corse clad in complete steel," "My father in his habit as he lived," etc., etc.—and the substitution for it of a sort of incandescent comet, from the neighborhood of which proceeded sepulchral sounds, barely recognizable as fragments of some of the most sonorous and effective blank verse ever provided for recitation. It is difficult to speak of such willful and senseless disregard and perversion of the text, with all its unmistakable implications, with even a pretence of civility. Art, for sooth! It was barbarous and childish.
>
> The acting, which ought to be the prime object of consideration . . . on this occasion, as in the precedent of "Macbeth," but to a less disastrous extent, seems to have been regarded as a matter entirely subordinate to the scenery. . . .[2]

Heywood Broun of the *World,* on the other hand, liked the production concept, except for one important scene:

> [Jones] has achieved height and solidity and yet there is opportunity for certain flexible variations. In effect, we

have "Hamlet" played on a vast staircase with three distinct stages. The set is the great hall of the palace, but at the back is a lofty arch through which we may see the sky. All the platform scenes are played just outside this arch.

The court scenes, of course are performed in the great hall, while others are played in front of a curtain on the wide apron of the stage. To our notion, only one episode mars the scheme. Ophelia is buried in the front parlor, which seems to us a mistake. It should not have been difficult to avoid this. The necessity of making a graveyard of the palace is not apparent. . . .

Visually we liked the ghost, who appears against the backdrop as a shrinking comet, but his voice does not come through effectively. The costuming and the grouping of the figures are admirable throughout. . . .[3]

The production was considered an important event deserving careful attention, and *New York Times* critic John Corbin devoted a long, penetrating article to it (and to the problem of staging Shakespeare) in the Sunday drama section:

"Hamlet" without the Play—A Tragedy

If John Barrymore fails to establish himself as the Hamlet of his generation, . . . it will not be for lack of endowment in physique and in inward genius, nor yet for the lack of faithful and intelligent study. . . . The worm i' th' bud of his fair hope is the setting which has been provided for him. This is the more remarkable—and probably, alas the more irremediable—because Arthur Hopkins is the most progressive and laudably ambitious of our managers, and Robert Edmond Jones the most renowned of our scenic artists. Yet between them they have snuffed out this drama. Sir Walter Scott's notion of billing the play of "Hamlet" without the Prince has become a proverb of fantastic humor. Mr. Barrymore has actually achieved Prince Hamlet without the play, and that is by way of being a tragedy.

It is true that the usual number of scenes are given, with a text unusually full. Verbally, Shakespeare receives due reverence. But something more is needful to drama than the reading of lines. . . . Let us proceed to an orderly diagnosis of symptoms.

Nothing is more fundamental in the dramatic structure than Hamlet's encounter with the Ghost. The Majesty of buried Denmark "enters" upon the stage "in his habits as he lived . . . a dread corse again in complete steel." . . . There can be no doubt as to Shakespeare's dramatic intention. Nor is there any doubt as to the effect; nine generations have thrilled to it. But the Ghost of Mr. Jones's imagination waivers fitfully against a silver-blue backdrop, some trillions of miles aloof in interstellar space, while the voice of the actor booms upstage right, from a definite spot behind a stage wall. Which is this Hamlet to face, the apparition or the voice? He cannot face either, if the audience is to read the suppressed terror in his lineaments. So he dodges, as it were, from one to another. Instead of the awe and inspiration of the actual encounter, steadily visible and dramatic, we have a patent absurdity. Why?

In the scene of the King at prayer, there is the contrary absurdity. Claudius kneels on an apron over the orchestra pit holding his crucifix to the noses of the unfortunate fold in the front row. Hamlet enters through a curtain just behind him, draws his sword and then pauses to discuss with himself whether he will do murder . . . in tones audible to the last row in the balcony; yet Claudius . . . does not hear. What is the matter with acting on the stage? Is there any imaginable reason why the Ghost is relegated to interstellar space while the King is required to rub noses with the audience?

The reason, such as it is, apparently lies in the new art of stage decoration. . . . In theory it is plausible enough. Scenery should give the mood of the play symbolically, in the manner of Gordon Craig. Thus the Tower of London dominated "Richard the Third." In "Macbeth" a dining-room screen snipped into the similitude of three Gothic arches, symbolized the castle of the Thane—and the public blames Lionel Barrymore for failure to create illusion! The symbol of "Hamlet" is a massive flight of steps flanked by two castle walls and leading up to the platform, beyond a high arch through which the heavens shine. . . . Mr. Jones's "symbol" has usurped the area needful to the creation of any genuine dramatic effect. One cannot play Shakespeare up and down stairs. So we have a Ghost entangled with the Pleiades and a King at his orisons, crucifix to nose with Broadway.

The devitalizing effect of this huge scenic symbol is subtle as it is gross. Thus Mr. Barrymore is obliged to play the "nunnery" scene with Ophelia far down stage and to one side; nowhere else is there a curtain available for the King and Polonius to hide behind. He carries the scene with consummate grace and passion. . . . But, thanks to these stairs, the scene is huddled in a corner. . . . In the scene of Ophelia's burial such incongruity reaches its climax of disillusionment. . . . the funeral procession perforce wends its way to the foot of those inevitable stairs, down front, where the grave-diggers have made a pit. At best the poor lady is buried in a courtyard, the thronged centre of the castle; but, as all of the presumable indoor scenes have occurred there, Heywood Broun is quite justified in saying that they planted her in the parlor. . . . The actors are doomed to forego the central playing space and nibble around the edges of Mr. Jones's front stoop like mice at a cheese. Drama is thrust out of the focus by this colossal impertinence of the scenic symbol. The Irving-Tree type of production, with its succession of shiftable scenes, was sufficiently devitalizing to the drama in all conscience, but it at least had the virtue of leaving the central playing space open to the actors. . . .

There was a time when Shakespeare's stage was said to have been small and bare . . . his stagecraft . . . primitive and crude. . . . For many decades now we have known that the Elizabethan stage was large . . . and that Shakespeare had at his command most of the resources of the modern theatre including scenery painted in perspective, if he chose to use it—which he did not. In proportion as he was an artist and a practical man of the theatre, his dramatic effects were presumably adapted to the conformation of his stage. To produce one of his plays without studying closely and intelligently its relation to this mold and matrix is as unscholarly as to use a garbled text or to disregard the matchless harmonies of his verse. It is far more likely to be fatal to illusion, to dramatic effect.

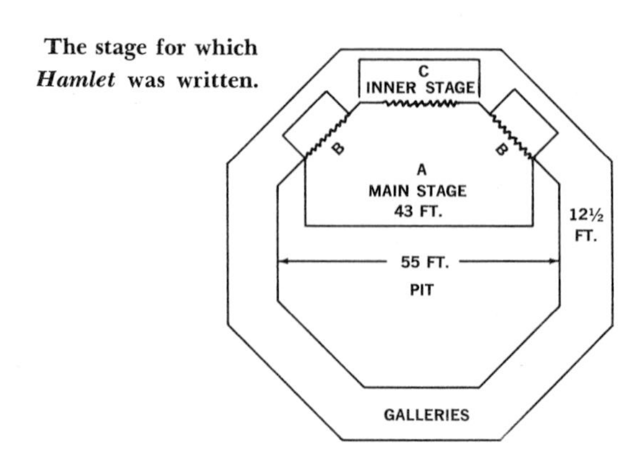

The stage for which *Hamlet* was written.

> The accompanying sketch gives the ground plan of the Elizabethan theatre. The octagonal form is that of Shakespeare's house, The Globe. The dimensions are from . . . the Fortune . . . modeled expressly after the Globe. All these details have been known to scholars for over one hundred years. . . . [a description of the use of the areas of the Globe stage follows, after which:]
>
> Note that Shakespeare's playing space occupied precisely the position usurped by Mr. Jones's "symbol." . . .
>
> It was to illustrate the dramaturgic value of this old stage that the New Theatre used it in 1911 to produce "The Winter's Tale" . . . [and thanks to it] . . . scored a success with both critics and public far beyond that of any of the Shakespearean productions in which they employed the marvelous mechanical and scenic resources of their theatre. In 1916 an Elizabethan stage was again used to produce "The Tempest." . . .
>
> It is not claimed that the old stage should be used for all productions of Shakespeare; far from it. . . . But to produce a drama regardless of Shakespeare's intention, sacrificing the main playing space . . . to the caprices of the scenic artist, is a work of sheer ignorance. . . . Any play of real merit—farce, comedy, or drama—is an artistic unit, deftly articulated in all its members and rhythmically measured in its flow. It is as rigidly subject to the laws of time and tone as a symphony. Only by treating it with due regard to its inner structure, its implicit harmonies, is it possible to release its rhythmic energies and make them assert their sway upon the minds and hearts of an audience. . . .[4]

This article brought a detailed reply, published in the "Drama Mailbag," from a distinguished friend and co-worker of Jones, Kenneth Macgowan:

Will you permit a fellow critic—who shares with you the enthusiasm of the opening night of Barrymore's "Hamlet" and of the review next day—to question certain points raised in the Sunday article? . . .

1. The Ghost—Obviously the will-of-the-wisp Ghost projected on the backdrop was a mistake. Shakespeare took as much pains to make the dialogue describe the dead King as he did to make it describe the locality of the action in many scenes in his plays. This might argue that the Ghost was no more visible to Elizabethan eyes than were the castle and forests of this sceneryless stage; but the general policy of Hopkins in keeping the Ghost invisible hardly needs any such defense. The mistake is obviously in presenting this Ghost at one point as a flickering luminous shape. I do not quarrel with you there.

2. The King at Prayer. You object to the King kneeling upon the forestage close to the audience. Do you think Shakespeare never used the front part of his far-projecting stage to bring his characters close to his audience? . . . Do you insist that the King be placed further away from Hamlet than the audience, in order that Hamlet may speak to the playgoer without the King overhearing? Do you imagine, finally, that Hamlet was actually speaking aloud in this scene? I had supposed it was his thoughts only that spoke. What, it might be asked, is an aside, anyway?

3. The Nunnery Scene—[brings us to the setting] Your general contention is that the "massive flight of steps" occupies "the central playing space." . . . You say that these steps force Hamlet and Ophelia to play "far down and to one side." I fail to see why playing far downstage is anything but desirable, and I venture to say that most of the playing in Shakespeare's own Globe was done far downstage. . . . I fail to see, equally, why playing to one side

is necessarily bad. . . . In discussing . . . Jones's setting it would have been well, I think, to have printed a diagram of the stage corresponding to your cut of the Globe theatre. [Here he gives measurements of the forestage, etc.] When . . . the larger stage is used with its permanent setting, there is about twenty feet of playing space, before the sharp rise of the steps. . . . The massive steps are themselves about six feet deep and perhaps five feet high. I do not think that these steps can be said to occupy the central playing floor. . . . Actually they occupy about one-fifth of the playing space. . . . it happens that the low slant of the auditorium throws almost all eyes below the level of the steps, and gives the steps rather more prominence than they might have in another house.

4. The Massive Steps. "One cannot play Shakespeare up and down stairs." Indeed, I venture to think, that is just where you can play him. He used a balcony himself to get certain vertical relationships. Anyone who has seen Leopold Jessner stage "Othello" and "Richard III," upon various arrangements of steps and platforms . . . knows what fine fluidity of movement and contrast of position they give him. All through Europe I saw steps used this summer with the finest effect. I should rather argue that Hopkins does not use his steps enough.

5. The Graveyard—and likewise the whole scheme of the setting. Manifestly, if you look at Jones's Romanesque background as a piece of scenery, a room, the graveyard in its centre becomes absurd. But so do most of the other scenes, for "Hamlet" does not pass in any one room of the castle. It happens that "Hamlet" did not pass in any room at all when Shakespeare gave it at the Globe. As you know, it passed in front of a permanent architectural form . . . part of the body of the theatre. . . . Now the virtue

> of Jones's scheme . . . is that he places on the modern stage a permanent architectural form to replace the old Shakespearean theatre and to bridge the gap between it and our use of scenery and proscenium. Its towering walls are merely a convention, something suggestive of time and mood (as Shakespeare's background did not have to be). Technically, with the aid of the curtain in front, it solves the problem of changing scenes. Spiritually, it backs up the action with a presence suggesting time and mood. The steps which are part of this background are placed there as an element in the design. . . . To return to the grave, it is obvious, of course, that if you think of the setting as an actual room, the grave becomes absurd. I don't see why anyone has to think of it thus. Jones might have eliminated the difficulty by putting heavy doors in the arched opening at the back . . . turning the setting . . . into an exterior. He chose, I imagine, to stick to an attempt to establish not only the notion of a permanent architectural (and to this extent Shakespearean) stage, But also the notion that the stage may be trying to turn away altogether from scenery and illusion, to become a platform in a playhouse of permanent fixed beauty. Such a playhouse belongs to the actor—just as the Greek theatre and the Shakespearean theatre did—not to the so-called scene painter.[5]

In a neighboring column were printed Corbin's comments on this letter of Macgowan, under the heading, "Tradition and 'Hamlet.' "

> One great virtue of an organized and permanent art theatre is that it serves as a repository of tradition. The word is often used to denote a dead convention, and it must be granted that the usage is not without warrant in experi-

ence. But beneath any convention, alive or dead, there is a live and significant fact. The importance of handing down such facts from generation to generation is revealed by Kenneth Macgowan's courteous and interesting discussion of Mr. Jones's "Hamlet."

Mr. Macgowan's ingenious surmises with regard to the Ghost would have been impossible if he had remembered that the part was not only played but was played by Shakespeare himself. Rowe relating that it was "the top of his performance." . . .

[With regard to the stairs] . . . The question is not primarily as to the extent of the space occupied . . . but rather as to their location, across the rear centre of the main stage. This makes the rear exit impossible and thrusts the two side exits downstage to the feet of the proscenium. . . . To anyone familiar with [Shakespeare's] stage it must be evident that the ineffectiveness of the multitude of scenes in Arthur Hopkins's production, especially the Ghost scenes and the "nunnery" scene, resulted from the fact that the illusion which is easily possible upstage, with curtained exits close at hand, is quite impossible in the high visibility of the forestage, from which a quick exit is impossible except as a feat of athletic sprinting. . . .

An "Aside" Spoken Forward

The question of Hamlet's "aside" when he encounters the King at prayer is easily answered. . . . Mr. Jones makes Hamlet talk aloud and in intense passion with his sword drawn and the King kneeling between the point of it and the audience. . . . For better or for worse, the soliloquy is a device against which we of today have a rooted prejudice. Why, then, intensify our difficulty by placing the King between the menacing avenger and his audience? There is no reason, obviously, except that Mr. Jones is already in possession of the space needed for the true staging of the scene—by virtue of squatter's sovereignty.

Mr. Macgowan is eloquent as to the beauty and effectiveness of differences of level in the playing space, citing Continental examples. It is a phenomenon well known not only to artistic stage managers but to the architects of house gardens and landscape gardens. It was also known to Shakespeare, who used it consistently—in the raising of the inner stage, in the use of the gallery above it as a wall and of the window above the side entrance as a balcony. . . . The producer who faithfully follows Shakespeare's staging . . . discovers beauties undreamed of. But the attempt to play . . . up and down the stairs in the manner Mr. Macgowan advocates would banish them all as surely as Mr. Jones has banished the majesty of buried Denmark to interstellar space and doomed Ophelia to be "planted in the parlor."

It is a curious fact that Shakespeare's stage and the stages of the great Spaniards and the classic Greeks, though they differed in size, were identical in dramaturgic principle. Is it altogether an accident that these stages, and these three alone, have produced supreme masterpieces of poetic drama? . . . It would be sad indeed if the world were bound fast in the dead tradition of their stagecraft, but it is equally sad that young men should dope themselves with the modern and mechanistic stagecraft of the Continent to the extent of ignoring the achievements of the supreme master of their own theatre and of the drama of the world.

Notes

FOREWORD AND INTRODUCTION

1. John Ciardi, "Poetry as Knowledge," *Saturday Review of Literature,* July 22, 1961, p. 39.

2. Michel Saint-Denis, *Theatre: The Rediscovery of Style,* Theatre Arts Books, Inc., New York, 1960, p. 70.

3. Directed by Orson Welles, designed by Nat Karson, for the Harlem division of the Federal Theatre, 1936. Photo: Culver Pictures, Inc.

4. A production by the Goodman Theatre of Chicago. Photo: American National Theatre and Academy.

5. Act. I, scene 1, Jean Vilar as Macbeth and Jean Deschamps as Banquo; a production by the Théâtre National Populaire, Avignon, 1954. See *Théâtre de France,* vol. V, 1955. Photo: Agnès Varda, Paris.

6. Designed by Robert Edmond Jones for the Arthur Hopkins production of 1921. Photo: Harvard Theatre Collection.

7. Directed and produced by Barry Jackson, Kingsway Theatre, London, 1925. Photo: Harvard Theatre Collection.

8. Directed by K. H. Hilar, designed by J. Hofman, for the Prague National Theatre, 1926. Photo: Karel Vana.

9. Directed and designed by Franco Zeffirelli, Rome, 1963. Photo: DeAntonis.

10. The Baylor University "Four-Faced *Hamlet,*" Waco, Texas, 1957. Photo: Myron Davis, *Life* magazine, © 1949, Time, Inc. All Rights Reserved.

11. Maurice Valency, "Flight into Lunacy," *Theatre Arts,* August, 1960, p. 9.

12. A Brattle Theatre production, Cambridge, Mass., 1950. Photo: Peter Rositer, Harvard Theatre Collection.

13. Designed by Isamu Noguchi, John Gielgud as Lear, The Palace Theatre, Stratford, 1955. Photo: Larry Burrows, *Life* magazine, © Time, Inc. All Rights Reserved.

14. "Role of Director Defined by Panel," *The New York Times,* Feb. 9, © 1960, p. 26. Reprinted by permission.

15. Quoted by Louis Jouvet in "The Profession of the Producer, II," *Theatre Arts,* January, 1937, p. 61.

16. Alan Dent (ed.), *Hamlet: The Film and the Play,* World Film Publications, London, 1948, Foreword, n.p.

17. "The Profession of the Producer, I," *Theatre Arts,* December, 1936, p. 949.

PART I

1. *The New Landscape,* Paul Theobald, Chicago, 1956, p. 41.

2. Doubleday & Company, Inc., Garden City, N. Y., 1954, pp. v-vii.

3. In more technical terms, this book defines metaphor as *implicit experiential analogy.* As long ago as 1923, Ernst Cassirer described metaphor as a conceptual process, a form of conceiving. He described the differences between metaphorical thinking and logical thought as follows:

> Logical contemplation always has to be carefully directed toward the extension of concepts; classical syllogistic logic is ultimately nothing but a system of rules for combining, subsuming and superimposing concepts. But the conceptions embodied in . . . [myth and art] must be taken not in extension, but in intension; not quantitatively, but qualitatively.
>
> *Language and Myth, trans. S. K. Langer,*
> *Dover Publications, Inc.*
> *New York, 1946, p. 91.*

In other words, the artistic meaning of a work of art (an

art work may also carry logical content) is in the effect of the total form.

4. Photo: Brogi-Art Reference Bureau.

5. The first stanza of one of his most famous sonnets; translation by the authors. For the full poem see Creighton Gilbert (trans.), *Complete Poems and Selected Letters of Michelangelo,* Random House, Inc., New York, 1963, p. 100.

6. Walter Sanders photo of Paris Opera House audience. *Life* magazine, © 1949, Time, Inc. All Rights Reserved.

7. Photo: Arthur Witman, *St. Louis Post Dispatch,* from Black Star Publishing Company, Inc.

8. Kabuki actor in *Sukeraku.* Photo: Courtesy of Consulate General of Japan.

9. Photo: Courtesy of the Museum of Modern Art Film Library.

10. T. B. L. Webster, *Greek Theatre Production,* Methuen & Co., Ltd., London, 1956, p. 4.

11. More than a hundred years after he wrote *The Way of the World* (1700) the actor-audience relationship for which Congreve wrote had not essentially changed—as this illustration by George Kruikshank shows. The drawing is from the early nineteenth century. Photo: Theatre Arts Books, Inc.

12. The Theatre of Epidaurus during a performance of Euripides' *Hecuba,* as performed by the National Theatre Organization, at the annual Festival of Ancient Greek Drama at Epidaurus. Photo: D. A. Harissiadis, Athens.

13. "Poseidon" or "Zeus." The statue is contemporary with Sophocles. Photo: Hirmer-Fotoarchiv, Munich.

14. From Ode I, *Antigone,* the translation of Fitts and Fitzgerald. See *The Oedipus Cycle of Sophocles,* Harcourt, Brace & World, Inc., New York, 1939.

15. Giacometti's "Man Pointing." Photo: Courtesy of the Trustees of the Tate Gallery.

16. "Tennessee Williams Presents His POV," *The New York Times,* June 12, 1960, sec. 6, p. 78. Reprinted by permission.

17. Lewis Funke and John Booth, *Actors Talk about Acting,* Random House, Inc., New York, 1961, pp. 416–417. Reprinted by permission of Random House, Inc.

18. *A Life in the Theatre,* McGraw-Hill Book Company, New York, 1959, pp. 234–235.

PART II

1. In a conversation quoted by Werner Haftmann, *The Mind and the Work of Paul Klee,* Faber and Faber, Ltd., London, 1954, p. 115. The translation used here is that of Gyorgy Kepes; Haftman's English rendering is slightly different.

2. W. M. Rossetti (ed), *The Poetical Works of Percy Bysshe Shelley,* E. Moxon, Son and Company, London, 1870, vol. I, p. 307. Italics added by the authors.

3. Browne's Bookstore, Chicago, p. 149.

4. Samuel French, Inc., New York, 1958, pp. 125–126.

5. Lewis Funke and John Booth, *Actors Talk about Acting,* Random House, Inc,, New York, 1961, p. 276. Reprinted by permission of Random House, Inc.

6. *Ibid.,* pp. 93–94.

7. Photo: By permission of Donald Oenslager.

8. *The New York Times,* Jan. 6, 1957, sec. 2, p. 7. Reprinted by permission.

9. Copyright, 1937, by Clifford Odets. Reprinted by

permission of Brandt and Brandt. Prompt-copy notations by the authors.

10. Designed by the authors of this book.

11. Adapted from Donald Oenslager's floor plan. By permission of Donald Oenslager.

12. Photo: Vandamn.

13. Lillian Ross, "Profiles," *The New Yorker,* Oct. 21, 1961, pp. 70–72. © 1961. Also included in Lillian Ross and Helen Ross, *The Player: A Profile of an Art,* Simon and Schuster, Inc., New York, 1963.

14. Photo: Collection of Mr. Wright Ludington.

15. "Taste in High Life." Photo: Print Collection, New York Public Library.

16. John Latouche, *Theatre Arts,* July, 1956, p. 80.

17. Act I, scene 1, "The Tabor Opera House." By permission of Donald Oenslager. Photo: Peter A. Juley and Son.

18. Act I, scene 3, "Augusta's Parlor." By permission of Donald Oenslager. Photo: Peter A. Juley and Son.

19. *The Architecture of Humanism,* Doubleday & Company, Inc., Garden City, N. Y., 1954, p. 168.

20. *Space, Time, and Architecture,* Harvard University Press, Cambridge, Mass., 1952, p. 19.

21. This and the following quotations from *Phèdre* are in the translation of Oreste F. Pucciani, *Jean Racine: Phèdre,* Appleton-Century-Crofts, Inc., New York, 1959.

22. University of California Press, Berkeley, Calif., 1952, p. 87.

23. In the Monastery Church, Rohr, Bavaria. Photo: Marburg-Art Reference Bureau.

24. Photo: The Bettmann Archive, Inc.

25. *Phèdre, de Jean Racine: Mise en scène et commentaires de Jean-Louis Barrault,* Editions du Seuil, Paris,

1946, p. 127. See also Toby Cole and Helen Krich Chinoy, *Directors on Directing,* The Bobbs-Merrill Company, Inc., Indianapolis, 1963, pp. 351–363.

26. North porch of the Erechtheum, Athens. Photo: Copyright Deutsches Archäologisches Institut, Athens.

27. Chapelle du Val de Grâce, Paris. Photo: H. Roger Viollet, Paris.

28. Quoted by Martin Turnell, *The Classical Moment,* New Directions, Norfolk, Conn., 1948, p. 180.

29. Photo: Eileen Darby, Graphic House.

30. A production at the National Theatre of Buenos Aires, 1952. Photo: By permission of Mario Vanarelli.

31. Model by Joseph Urban for a production at the Metropolitan Opera House. See *Theatre Arts Prints, Series II,* Theatre Arts, Inc., New York, n.d., Plate 38.

32. From "The Provincetown Playbill," Provincetown Playhouse.

33. Photo: Courtesy of the Museum of Modern Art.

34. Photo: Courtesy Mordecai Gorelik.

35. "Designing the Play" in John Gassner, *Producing the Play,* The Dryden Press, Inc., New York, 1953, p. 354.

36. Photo: Bruguière, courtesy of the Theatre Division, New York Public Library.

37. "The God of Stumps," *The Nation,* Nov. 26, 1924, p. 578.

38. Toby Cole and Helen Krich Chinoy, *Directors on Directing,* The Bobbs-Merrill Company, Inc., Indianapolis, 1963, p. 222.

39. *Ibid.,* "An Audience of One," p. 248.

40. "The Play of Ideas," *Theatre Arts,* August, 1950, p. 17.

41. Design by Daniel Krempel.

42. Maurice Zolotow, " 'Ulysses' on Houston Street,"

The New York Times, June 1, 1958, sec. 2, p. 3. Reprinted by permission.

PART III

1. "The Hero as King," *Carlyle's Complete Works,* Dana Estes and Charles E. Lauriat, Boston, 1884, vol. I, p. 425.

2. *What is Theatre?,* Beacon Press, Boston, 1956, pp. 60–61.

3. *World Theatre,* vol. 10, no. 3, p. 204, Autumn, 1961.

4. "Designing the Play" in John Gassner, *Producing the Play,* The Dryden Press, Inc., New York, 1953, pp. 310–311.

5. Production at Le Petit Théâtre du Vieux Carré in conjunction with Tulane University. Photo: Courtesy of Monroe Lippman.

6. A Gothenburg Municipal Theatre Production, 1944. Photo: Courtesy of the Swedish Institute, lent by the Theatre Museum of Gothenburg.

7. "Introduction," *Arthur Miller's Collected Plays,* The Viking Press, Inc., New York, 1957, pp. 26–27. This essay also appears in Toby Cole (ed.), *Playwrights on Playwriting,* Hill and Wang, Inc., New York, 1960, p. 264.

PART IV

1. *Theaterarbeit,* VVV Dresdner Verlag, Dresden, 1952, p. 310. See also Cole and Chinoy, *Directors on Directing,*

The Bobbs-Merrill Company, Inc., Indianapolis, 1963, p. 348.

2. Photo: Gjon Mili.

3. Ralph Pendleton (ed.), *The Theatre of Robert Edmond Jones,* Wesleyan University Press, Middletown, 1958, pp. 5–6.

4. The sleepwalking scene, Act V, scene 1. Photo: Courtesy of Mrs. Honor Leeming Luttgen.

5. This unidentified item is quoted from a large file of newspaper clippings on the "Barrymore *Hamlet*" in the Harvard Theatre Collection. The sources of some of these clippings can be identified, but others are untraceable. Subsequent references to this file are designated "Harvard."

6. *The New Republic,* Dec. 6, 1922, p. 46.

7. "Barrymore Is Cheered When He Plays 'Hamlet'," *New York Sun,* Nov. 17, 1922, n.p., Harvard.

8. "It Seems To Me," *New York World,* Nov. 18, 1922, n.p., Harvard.

9. John Corbin, "Hamlet without the Play: A Tragedy," *The New York Times,* Nov. 26, 1922, sec. 8, p. 1. Reprinted by permission.

10. Photo: Courtesy of Mrs. W. E. Pennington.

11. Reproduced from Robert Edmond Jones, *Drawings for the Theatre,* Theatre Arts, Inc., New York, 1925, Plate 23. Present owner of the design could not be discovered.

12. *Ibid.*

13. "In the Mail Bag," *The New York Times,* Dec. 10, 1922, sec. 8, p. 1. Reprinted by permission.

14. Harvard.

15. "Hamlet Spectacle and Little Else," *New York Evening Post,* Nov. 17, 1922, n.p., Harvard.

16. Corbin, *loc. cit.*

17. Jones, *op. cit.*, p. 16.

18. *New York Evening Post,* n.d., Harvard.

19. *How's Your Second Act?* Philip Goodman, New York, 1918, p. 24. *Italics added.*

20. Who, appropriately, once contended that *Hamlet* was not a play to be performed, but only to be read, and that the true theatre art of Elizabethan England was to be found in the court masques and pageants. See *On the Art of the Theatre,* Browne's Bookstore, Chicago, 1911, p. 143.

21. *A Life in the Theatre,* McGraw-Hill Book Company, New York, 1959, p. 207.

22. By permission of the Stratford Shakespearean Festival. Photo: Peter Smith.

23. The play was produced at the Westminster, directed by Michael Macowan.

24. "A Song." Photo: Angus McBean, London.

25. "Cressida Leaves Troy." Photo: Angus McBean, London.

26. "The Trojan Palace." Photo: Huston Rogers, London.

27. "The Departure of Hector." Photo: Huston Rogers, London.

28. "Helen of Troy." Photo: Huston Rogers, London.

29. Reprinted with permission of *Playbill,* the magazine for theatregoers.

30. "The Court." Photo: Angus McBean, London.

31. Tom Driver, " 'As Flies to Wanton Boys'," *The Reporter,* Mar. 14, 1963, p. 45.

32. "The Triumph of Stratford's Lear," *The Observer Weekend Review,* Nov. 11, 1962, p. 26.

33. "Double Will from England," *Time,* May 29, 1964, p. 49.

34. "Lear Log," *Tulane Drama Review,* vol. 8, no. 8, p. 104, Winter 1963.

35. "Goneril's Palace." Photo: Angus McBean, London.

36. Harold Clurman, "Theatre," *The Nation,* Jan. 26, 1963, p. 77.

37. Harold Hobson, "A Vengeful Universe," *The Sunday Times Magazine* [London], Nov. 11, 1962, p. 41.

38. Walter Kerr, " 'King Lear' from England," *New York Herald Tribune,* May 19, 1964, p. 20.

39. *Ibid.*

40. J. C. Trewin, "Royal and Ancient," *The Illustrated London News,* Nov. 17, 1962, p. 804.

41. Robert Brustein, "Shakespeare with a Few Tears," *The New Republic,* Jan. 13, 1964, p. 31.

42. Hobson, *loc. cit.*

43. Clurman, *loc. cit.*

44. Bomber Gascoign, "Unhappy Families," *The Spectator,* Dec. 21, 1962, p. 966.

45. Kerr, *loc. cit.*

46. Driver, *loc. cit.*

47. Clurman, *loc. cit.*

48. Brustein, *op. cit.,* p. 32.

PART V

1. Bohdan Korzeniewski, quoted in "Rights and Duties of the Producer," *World Theatre,* vol. 10, no. 3, p. 204, Autumn, 1961.

2. "They're Cultural, but Are They Cultured?" *The New York Times,* July 9, 1961, sec. 6, p. 37. Reprinted by permission.

APPENDIX A

1. "Faery Palace." Photo: Culver Pictures, Inc.

2. "Pyramus and Thisbe." Photo: Culver Pictures, Inc.

3. "A Priest." Photo: Culver Pictures, Inc.

4. "Dunsinane." Photo: Culver Pictures, Inc.

5. Alan Dent (ed.), *Hamlet: The Film and the Play,* World Film Publications, London, 1948, Foreword, n.p.

6. Peter Alexander, *Hamlet, Father and Son,* Oxford University Press, Fair Lawn, N. J., 1955.

7. "The Queen's Chamber." Photo: Courtesy of The Museum of Modern Art Film Library.

8. "Pursuing the Ghost." Photo: Courtesy of The Museum of Modern Art Film Library.

APPENDIX C

1. C. C. L. Gregory and Anita Koshen, *Physical and Psychical Research,* The Omega Press, Surrey, 1954, p. 16.

2. R. J. Hefferline, "Communication Theory: I. Integrator of the Arts and Sciences," *Quarterly Journal of Speech,* vol. 41, p. 223, October, 1955.

3. Albert Einstein, "Autobiographical Notes," trans. Arthur Schilpp, *Albert Einstein: Philosopher Scientist,* Library of Living Philosophers, Evanston, 1949, p. 13.

4. Ernst Cassirer, *Language and Myth,* trans. S. K. Langer, Dover Publications, Inc., New York, 1946, p. 8.

5. Bernard C. Heyl, *New Bearings in Aesthetics and Art Criticism,* Yale University Press, New Haven, Conn., 1943, pp. 5, 84.

6. Gyorgy Kepes, *Language of Vision,* Paul Theobald, Chicago, 1944, pp. 13, 16.

7. Rudolph Arnheim, *Art and Visual Perception,* University of California Press, Berkeley, Calif., 1954, p. 374.

8. Harvard University Press, Cambridge, Mass.

9. *Feeling and Form* and *Problems of Art* both by Charles Scribner's Sons, New York.

APPENDIX D

1. Nov. 17, 1922, n.p., Harvard. See Note 5, Part IV, for explanation

2. Nov 17, 1922, n.p., Harvard.

3. "It Seems To Me," Nov. 18, 1922, n.p., Harvard.

4. Nov. 26, 1922, sec. 8, p. 1. Reprinted by permission.

5. *The New York Times,* Dec. 10, 1922, sec. 8, p. 1. Reprinted by permission.

Index